D
Christmas Diary

David Street's Christmas Diary

Martin Saunders

Authentic
LIFESTYLE

First published 2003 by Authentic Lifestyle

09 08 07 06 05 04 03   7 6 5 4 3 2 1

Authentic Lifestyle is a division of Authentic Media,
9 Holdom Avenue, Bletchley, Milton Keynes, Bucks,
MK1 1QR, UK

Distributed in the USA by Gabriel Resources,
P.O. Box 1047, Waynesboro, GA 30830-2047, USA

British Library Cataloguing in Publication Data
A catalogue record for this book is available from
the British Library.

1-86024-439-4

Cover illustration by Al Gray
Cover design by David Lund
Typeset by WestKey Limited, Falmouth, Cornwall
Printed in Denmark by Nørhaven Paperback

For
Barbara and Kath

ACKNOWLEDGEMENTS

Thanks to Steve Adams, John Karter, Keith Saunders and Trevor Smith for all your help in writing and re-writing.

With extra special thanks to my good friend Andy Peck. Without you, your advice, and all those cups of coffee, this book would not have come into being.

Monday
1st December

Now let's establish something from the start. I don't like you.

It's nothing personal, you understand. But a combination of factors means that a friendship between us would be, at best, implausible. For a start, I'm only holding you in my hands right now because you were passed on to me by my insane ex-wife – a woman placed on this earth solely for the purpose of my continued mental and emotional torment. You were left on the porch, under the guise of a loving early Christmas present, as a token of her hatred, and as a rather smarmy attempt at asserting her authority as 'the one who got over us quickest'.

You are, if you'll excuse the pun, only the latest chapter in an ongoing saga of patronising and vividly-illustrated literary put-downs that have been levelled in my direction since our acrimonious split of 35 months ago, the legacy of which stretches back some way before that. Before you there was *Rebuilding Your Shattered Life, Self-esteem for the Hurting*, and *I Am Man, Hear Me Roar*. You were barely a twinkle in a marketing man's eye when this war started, Mr so-called 'Christmas Diary'. If that is your real name.

You are, as a gift you see, inseparably bonded to the giver who gave you. And in your case, that means you are, in my mind at least, welded to the memory of the worst thing in the world. In fact you may well wonder why on earth I'm wasting my time with you at all. If so, good question. Well, unlike the company that manufactured you for the fastest buck going, I have values. And when my daughter, the light of my rather jaded life, begs me to do something for her, I'm often inclined to relent, even against my own better judgement. And of course, as a side effect, you'll provide helpful ammunition next time I have to speak to the 'Evil One'. You see, once your pages have been filled with the outpourings of my cynical mind, my failure to be helped by her self-help handouts will neatly deflect her attempts to win this latest bout of one-upmanship.

I also refuse to like you on the grounds that you are probably the most disgracefully cynical piece of seasonal exploitation it has ever been my gross misfortune to trip over. It may interest you – presuming that you were once happy as a tree somewhere, providing an effective basis for a complete ecosystem – that your life was prematurely ceased so that you could end your days as part of the Magico™ 'True Meaning of

Christmas Gift Set'. According to the words written on the remains of one of your former forest colleagues – a jagged bookmark stuffed inside your front cover – you are intended to 'help me to help myself' in 'rediscovering the reason for the season'. Which, frankly, makes me want to puke.

Thirdly, and perhaps most importantly of all, I am completely unable to like you on the grounds that you are, by nature, inescapably Christmas-related. And I really, really hate Christmas.

So, now that we've got that straight, shall we begin? On second thoughts, Bianca's just got home from school. Don't want her thinking that her dad's gone soft or she'll have a non-drop tree in the corner quicker than I can say 'humbug'. And with all my years of practice, I can say it pretty quick. I'll start tomorrow.

Tuesday
2nd December

It begins. Twenty-three days until that God-forsaken day, and already we have our first card. It's from Great Aunt Betty, who I haven't seen for twenty-four years, and who I'm only likely to see again if she finally carries out her decades-old threat to streak at the rugby. Perhaps that explains the inscription – pre-printed of course – which sums up almost quintessentially the lack of effort which one only reserves for one's least favourite relatives. I quote:

> Just a little festive wish
> To send you lots of cheer
> A very merry Christmas,
> And a really great New Year

If I ever meet the man who devised that message, I'm going to perform a prefrontal lobotomy on him with a rusty fork and a wooden spoon. Although, on second thoughts, the only minds capable of such drivel have probably already been lobotomised several times over. I mean, does Great Aunt Betty genuinely want to wish me a 'really great' New Year? Wouldn't she rather it was a 'happy' one? Aha I hear you cry – but that would have messed up the rhyme pattern and left us one beat short! So it had to be 'really great' instead, which all sounds terribly half-hearted and makes me think that if I fell under a bus tomorrow morning, Great Aunt Betty would only think it was 'really quite a shame'.

In all the excitement of yesterday, I forgot to mention the other tip-top components which make up the Magico™ 'True Meaning of Christmas Gift Set'. Aside from you, Mr Twelfth-of-a-real-diary, there's also a quite marvellous talking advent calendar, which, as far as I can ascertain, features the voice of a top celebrity (note: some voices may be impersonated) behind every single door. And a picture of some holly! I'm sure I'll barely be able to get to sleep each night with the adrenaline-fuelled excitement of what the next day's panel might bring.

There are also a number of fillers, presumably placed with the more substantial items in order to raise the price a bit. Four crackers, some paper decorations, a couple of cardboard hats and one of those extendable paper whistle things that make normally-docile pets viciously attack you.

Last but not least – oh joy – at the bottom of the well-padded box I've found a piece of paper with a list of 'Ten Things to Make Your Christmas Great' printed on one side. More on this later, if I can be bothered.

Talking of which, this morning Bianca, the oh-so-sweet apple of my rotten eye, presented me with this year's ransom demand. She calls it a letter to Santa, but we'll agree to differ on that one. Once again she has demonstrated either that she completely misunderstands our current financial position and hasn't noticed that we've had to convert our house into a Bed & Breakfast simply to make ends meet, or else she sees her father as some latter day miracle-man, capable of extracting blood from a stone and a Nagatoshi Gamemaster from an empty bank account. Either way, she knows that a document of this nature is never popular with her ever-loving father, which may explain why she left it under the windscreen wiper on my car before heading off to school in the manner of a Canadian short-distance runner. I presume that she knows that Santa doesn't drive a bottom-of-the-range three-door runabout, and placed it there because she thinks that I must have more direct contact details, but then they do say that educational standards are slipping.

Anyhow, to give her credit, the tactical deployment of this bombshell was not unintelligent. Had she asked me for Nagatoshi Gamemaster outright, face to face as a show of respect, I would have laughed, ranted and said no. As it is, I've had time to boil, simmer, and cool down. I'll look into how much they cost and see if I can do a bit of creative accounting.

I'm thankful for small mercies anyway, and at least she's lowered her horizons a little. Last year she asked for a pony.

Now just before we really get stuck in to the thing I hate most in the entire world, let me spend a moment on the one thing that I care about. You see – life's dealt me a pretty unfair hand, as I'm sure you'll find out over the next few weeks. But despite my failed marriage, my failed career and my failed happiness, I have been granted just one flickering illumination in all the gloom. Her name is Bianca, she's thirteen years old, and she's absolutely perfect in every way. She was born into the happiest moment of my life, and her face is a lasting monument to it. I may be a downbeat thirty-something failure, but Bianca is my one success. And though sometimes I might misunderstand her, and sometimes she might misunderstand me (Ransom notes being a good example), I love her, completely, unconditionally, and like nothing else.

So if I sound a little negative at times, don't assume (as much as a dead piece of paper can make assumptions) that it's because I'm wallowing in my own self-pity. It's also because I see the world that my perfect little girl is growing up in. It's dark, and dirty, and imperfect, and whilst it might be all I deserve, it's not good enough for her. And Christmas, or rather the horror that we now call Christmas, is the darkest, dirtiest part of it all.

Wednesday
3rd December

Well I hope you're impressed. Three days into the month and I'm still writing, meaning that I've beaten my all-time diary-keeping stickablility record. It has beaten the long-time champion – 'Diary of a Happy Marriage' – by a whole day. You should feel proud, although I guess you probably can't get over the fact that as a former tree you could have been something so much more useful. Like a toilet roll.

With you in mind, I've been watching the actions of our next-door neighbours. Unlike me, the head of their family has a nice job – bank manager or something similar I think – and hence they don't have to rent out their spare bedrooms to complete strangers. Nice bloke though: pays his taxes and returns borrowed gardening equipment; so I'm not bitter. All in all they're a perfectly normal family.

Or at least, for eleven months of the year they are. When December comes around, they all turn very strange, just for a month. Decorations to befit the Eiffel Tower . . . a horde of presents big enough to make an American teenager whinge with jealousy . . . and don't even get me started on the singing. Suddenly, after over 330 days of normal, average, bona fide behaviour, they turn into the Brady Bunch Seasonal Special.

I thought they might provide an interesting reference and comparison point for you while I explain how a more sane person, like me, approaches the same lunar cycle.

You'll be pleased to hear that the talking advent calendar made its long-overdue debut on the shelf today, although only after great persistence from my tenacious daughter. Just in case you're interested, today's window revealed the poorly-impersonated voice of some two-bit kids TV presenter who I'd never heard of, but whose catch-phrase is apparently 'Wacktastic'. I know this because he wished me a 'Wacktastic Christmas' this morning. I shall of course try hard to crowbar that word into conversation wherever possible from now on.

Bookings for the B & B are beginning to pick up, as they tend to at this point every year, proving the popular theory that the only good thing that can come out of Christmas these days is a decent profit. For the past two weeks I've had an odd-smelling woman practically locked up in the downstairs bedroom, but apart from that things have been pretty slow. Tomorrow though, a Mr Hector Malone arrives for a week, and then from Saturday three doctors have booked themselves in until January. A full house then, for the first time all year. Wacktastic!

Disgusted. Because after opening today's advent window with a mixture of excitement and expectation – honest – I found that instead of the promised celebrity Christmas wish (note: some voices may be impersonated), door number four actually hides an advertisement for Magna Cola, which, an unrecognisable voice gurglingly informed me, will help me to have a 'bubbly Christmas'. Disappointed, I sat down immediately and gave this some serious thought. I realised three things. First: I see no reason why I should want to have a 'bubbly' Christmas. Bubbles are a miracle of nature: a beautiful little detail that helps to make the rest of our concreted world slightly less dull. However, they have absolutely no festive significance at all, and while obviously I'm very fond of bubbles, that passion operates on a year-round basis, and doesn't suffer any significant fluctuation over the Yuletide period. Second: the people at Magico™ are far more despicable than even I had given them credit for. Not only do they pump out poor-quality seasonal tat to unsuspecting simpletons, but they are also lying about their motivation for doing so. The big (well-padded) box, in which you and your companions arrived, clearly proclaimed that it was here 'to help me'. This blatantly isn't the case though, unless the people at Magico™ mistakenly think that I own shares in a soft drinks giant. Third: I shall no longer buy or drink Magna Cola. It gives me chronic wind anyway, but this display of cynicism really is the last straw.

Disgusted. Because after looking again at Bianca's Christmas list, I realised that I had only been looking at the front. The request to 'Santa' for a Nagatoshi Gamemaster was simply the tip of a rather large iceberg. On the other side of the paper, penned in slightly shaky handwriting by a girl clearly made nervous by the size of her cheek, is the kind of list which a man might well expect to receive from his teenage daughter. If he happened to be the Sultan of Brunei. Music, videos, clothes, make-up, car. I'm presuming, since Bianca is 13 years old, that the last item is a joke. But that's only a presumption. I intensely dislike saying this but, at least in terms of her unrealistic and cripplingly-expensive taste, Bianca certainly takes after her mother.

Disgusted. Because after returning from a spying trip in which I watched my temporarily-possessed neighbours erect an eight-foot effigy of Father Christmas on their front lawn, I received a phone message which made me swear and curse quite a bit. It was from the Princess of Darkness, and a transcript follows:

'Hello David, it's Louisa here. Just calling to see what you made of my little gift, but it seems you're not in. Are you ignoring the phone today, or just spying on the family next door again? I'm presuming, due to the time of year, that it's probably the latter. Anyway, hope you liked the gift set, and that it helps you to get through what's usually a tough time for you. Give me a call if you fancy a chat, which you won't, and give my love to B. Tell her she's still welcome to pop round whenever she's ready. Happy Christmas David.' Beep.

She didn't say 'beep' by the way, that was the machine. But how dare she leave such a condescending message? It may be a tough time for me, but I'm sure it's hardly a bed of roses for her either – preparing a Christmas lunch for one, disowned by her only daughter (who won't 'pop round') and almost certainly snowed under by bits of paper with numbers on. If she didn't have to be so hard-skinned about it, I'd probably have given her a call back. As it is she'll just have to sit there and feel smug, whilst drinking medically prohibited levels of coffee and reading *Miss Consultant* magazine.

Disgusted. Because after bravely venturing through the door of the odd-smelling woman's room this afternoon, I found that while the odd smell remains, the woman has evaporated, accidentally forgetting to pay for the last three days of her stay. And if there's one thing I hate more than anything – even Christmas – it's people who get away without paying. Although as something of a conciliatory bonus, she appears not to have used up any of the complimentary shower gel. Which, when you think about it, doesn't come as so much of a surprise.

It dances! Dear God! The eight-foot effigy of Father Christmas dances! It wiggles inanely from back to front, then from side to side, like some mad child with an imaginary hula-hoop. To classic Christmas tunes from the 70s!

I'm standing in front of the house this morning, casually spying on some of my other neighbours, when Geoff, the guy next door, calls me over.

'David!' he says. 'Do you want to see something cool?'

Somehow I manage to conceal my distaste for middle-aged people who use words like 'cool'.

'OK!' I chirpily reply.

'I know how much you love our little display each year!' he laughs, blissfully unaware that I'm picturing him electrocuting himself.

'Yes,' I say.

'Well, this is our crowning glory!'

'I saw your big Santa yesterday.'

'Yes David, but have you seen this?' he asks, with the kind of smugness that only comes from being completely ignorant of how stupid the eight-foot robot in your garden looks.

And then it happens. Geoff presses a little button on the side of Robo-Santa, and after a couple of whirring noises, it begins to lurch in three different directions at once. A little belatedly, some speakers hidden in Geoff's flowerbed begin to blurt out three verses of 'Santa Wants to Rock 'n' Roll'. I swear under my breath, perhaps slightly too loud, but Geoff is too wrapped up in his own personal Lapland to hear me.

'Had you seen that?' asks Geoff, with a face like a half-moon, and, quite incredibly, dancing with less co-ordination than the robot.

'No Geoff. I hadn't seen that. That's wacktastic!'

Mr Hector Malone arrived this afternoon, and I must admit that he went some way towards rebuilding my confidence in humankind (after Geoff had earlier taken a sledgehammer to it). These days it's quite normal for a guest to no-show. It's so common in fact, that readers of industry bible *Your House, Their Home* voted it the number one most irritating aspect of running a B & B. So when Mr Malone didn't turn up yesterday, I naturally assumed that he'd 'number one-d' all over me. But I was mistaken. Not only did he book in to the guesthouse today AND pay for a full week in advance, he also insisted that he compensated me for his mistake in booking the wrong date. Nice guy.

I told Bianca about her mother's message this evening, while we were enjoying our Friday night 'quality time' (fish and chips in front of a small flickering television). As I predicted, she was pretty unimpressed by the suggestion that she might want to go round to visit. She just sat in her chair, rolled her eyes and chuckled. For a start that upset me because I suddenly realised that she wasn't curled up in my lap, like she had been every Friday night for the last three years. More importantly, her response was a bit too grown-up and worldly for my liking, and so, through a mouthful of over-cooked chips, I suddenly found myself doing the unthinkable:

'Why don't you just give her half an hour?' I said, before choking. Where on earth had that come from?

'What? Are you feeling alright Dad?'

To be honest, I wasn't sure. Perhaps Mr Wong at the chip shop had grown bored with his traditional recipe and thrown a bit of vodka into the batter this evening. I thought hard before replying.

'I'm fine. I just think that, after three years, maybe you should sit down with her and swap Christmas cards.'

'Are you OK?'

I clearly wasn't OK. I didn't believe a word I was saying. Louisa had ripped this family apart, and I knew that Bianca was better off here with her dad. Yet seeing her just then, looking as cynical and resigned and hard-hearted as her father, made me ache. I felt suddenly more sober. Which cleared Mr Wong of any batter-tampering accusations.

'Don't avoid your mother on my account' seemed like the most mature and caring thing to say.

'You're an idiot' seemed like an unlikely reply, and that's probably why it stung so much as she stormed past me en-route to her room.

Christmas Day, three years ago, was the worst day of my life. We'd just bought this house, at a stretch, for the exclusive purpose of living in it. It was expensive, but since Louisa had just been promoted, and my sales job had recently brought in a healthy lump of commission, we decided to take a risk and invest. Then on Christmas Eve, filled with festive spirit, my family-friendly firm decided to jettison me with only a very small parachute attached. I plummeted home to Louisa, who was about as supportive as a leaky waterbed. We argued, bickered, shouted, rowed and screamed for about twenty-four hours on and off, until one of us noticed Bianca, crying in the corner. We stopped, and looked at each other, completely broken. In that instant, life could have headed in one of two ways, and though we both held the power, I let her decide.

'I'm leaving you,' said Louisa.

Which shattered Bianca's heart. Had it been me that had spoken those three words, then in all probability a 13-year-old girl would have just called her mother an idiot before slamming the door of her room in a different house. As it was, Louisa made a bad impression on Bianca which went a mile deep, and thus it was she who took all the blame for the way things fell apart.

I gave Bianca an hour before knocking at her door. She apologised for calling me an idiot, but kept her distance. I sat at the end of her bed for a while, trying to find something to say, but nothing came, and so I made my excuses and left. Then I sat on the end of my bed for a while, and tried to find something to get angry about. But nothing came, so I cried instead.

Saturday
6th December

Note to self: never begin to like or trust a man who helps to rebuild your shattered confidence in mankind. He's probably the devil in disguise.

I'd taken a liking to Mr Hector Malone (I don't know why I keep prefixing his name with a title, but it seems to make the word 'Hector' look slightly less ridiculous). He seemed like my sort of chap – affable, generous and honest. Indeed, as I served him his first breakfast this morning, I was almost overcome by his manner. From early impressions, he appeared to be a large four-pint carton on legs, filled to the brim with the milk of human kindness.

'Good morning Mr Street' said Hector, as he returned, slightly reddened, from his morning jog. He had a copy of *The Daily Spectacle* under his arm, which instantly set him apart as a man of letters.

'Good morning Mr Malone,' I replied, looking slightly less intellectual in my 'kiss-me-quick' cooking apron. 'Full English?'

'No!' he replied, bullet-quick. 'I'm half-Irish actually. And I'll have the smoked salmon and scrambled eggs please.'

Wit and class, displayed in a momentary flash, and so early in the day. I was amazed – we were rarely privileged with a guest of such distinction at the Streets Ahead Guesthouse. It was such a shame that he had to undo all that good work with a single word. Well, not so much a word even – more of an utterance:

'Ooh!' he exclaimed suddenly, nearly spilling his orange juice. 'You've got one of mine! You've got one of my works!'

I looked around the room for a minute, wondering what he was talking about. It made sense of course that this man was some sort of artist – he certainly had the air of a creative genius about him. But to what was he referring? I glanced at some of the pictures on our dining room wall. Monet, Van Gogh, B. Street aged six – none of them fitted the profile (unless Bianca had lied to us about drawing a three-legged cow, and Hector was a really rubbish artist). My gaze wandered to our rocking-chair, which Louisa specially commissioned to some famous woodworker who charges four times what he should and markets directly to overpaid management consultants with taste straight out of a style magazine. If that was Hector, I didn't know whether to punch him or hug him. But before I had a chance to decide, the man for whom I was developing such fondness offered chilling clarification. I saw what he was looking at. It was Great Aunt Betty's Christmas card.

The emotional tenseness of last night did not seem apparent in Bianca today as she buzzed her way through Saturday chores. She smiled sweetly as she cleared Mr Malone's breakfast dishes, made polite conversation with an old man who wandered into our kitchen off the street by mistake, and even displayed a sudden penchant for singing as she worked. Quite surprisingly, she seemed rather happy. On recent Saturdays I've noticed that she has taken more and more of an interest in the guesthouse, as if the added responsibility it brings allows her to shrug off her twin life as a schoolgirl. She may be 13, and it may technically be slave labour, but at the moment she really seems to enjoy it. In fact, she's really throwing herself in to it. This afternoon she booked our three new guests in without even telling me. She's never done that before. I think she may be looking for a promotion.

I suppose it was always likely to happen. We may call ourselves the 'Streets Ahead Guesthouse', but the idea was Bianca's, not mine. She came up with the whole thing about a year and a half ago, when we realised that Louisa's (admittedly mammoth) maintenance payments weren't quite covering the bills. We needed a top-up, and since my job-hunting efforts had proved as fruitless as a steak pie, we decided to employ a bit of lateral thinking.

We had a chat one night, after realising that we'd run out of buy-one-get-one-free pizza vouchers.

She said: 'We have a very big empty house, don't we Dad?'

I said: 'Yes darling, but that's because your mother ran out on us and took half of the furniture.' Obviously I wasn't completely over the break-up at that time.

She said: 'We should get some people to stay in the other rooms and give us money.'

I said: 'Let's get a lodger.'

She said: 'No, because Denzel White's dad got a lodger, and one day he stole their car.'

I said: 'I don't mind, my car is rubbish. That's your mother's fault too.'

She said: 'Let's turn it into a hotel.'

And I said: 'OK.'

So that's what we did. To be honest, at that time I was more interested in dreaming up imaginative forms of revenge than wasting valuable brain time by thinking through the feasibility of child-sourced business plans. Starting up a little company gave me something to do with my days, and I soon got into it. Bianca then took something of a back seat, as great visionaries often do, but within a month we were up and running, with a crass neon sign outside and headed notepaper on the desk. Admittedly the headed notepaper was delivered with one tiny spelling mistake, but we learned to see the positives: we got 30 per cent off the bill, and we now get to send out letters from the Street's Ahead Ghosthouse, which brings in a lot of extra trade around the end of October.

The brain behind the corporation has always kept her fingers in the pie though – mainly through the cleaning and clearing-up jobs for which I pay her 50p a day. I've always figured that she'd eventually head in one of two directions, and since she's still too young to join a trade union, I guess she's decided that it's time to take over instead. I'll be keeping my eye on that little careerist.

Well I still don't like you. And just because I've
filled you in every day, don't think that means
anything. You still represent a mocking gesture
from the evil one, and I'm still writing about
how utterly detestable this time of year is. You
are not therapy. You and the talking advent calendar (got that Welsh singer with the hairy
chest this morning – too old for the clothes he
wears; make-up always crumbling – I can never
remember his name) are teaching me nothing
positive about the meaning of Christmas – true,
false or otherwise. You are helping me, quite
ironically, to prove your worthlessness.

I will concede however, that I am enjoying
the writing process, not least because it gives me
something to do. I spend about an hour, every
night after the news, scribbling across your
pages, which means that generally now I only
spend around twenty-three hours doing
nothing each day. This is a marked improve-
ment, and you should be proud. Perhaps when
I've thrown you on a fire somewhere, I'll invest
in a real diary.

I've never met our local vicar, but I expect there are few things that we agree on. Though after the experience of today, I'm sure that we might find some common ground on the issue of Sunday trading.

I did a bit of clever accounts work yesterday (or, to be more accurate, I got our new guests to pay for the week ahead in cash) in order that this afternoon I might engage in some very intelligent Christmas shopping. My plan was very simple: go into town on the least busy day of the week, and nearly twenty days before the rest of the world suddenly remembers what time of year it is. So I got up, made Mr Malone's breakfast, and left my new assistant manager in charge of the late risers. I was in the car by ten, and it looked as if I'd be back home, with a Nagatoshi Gamemaster under my arm, by eleven-thirty. On paper it looked as if my perennial nightmare might for once be avoided.

That hope was shredded as soon as I got on to the ring road. A tailback worthy of a bi-annual rock festival was snaking all the way to the town centre, and on the radio, the inane bloke who does a couple of minutes between the adverts was reporting 'record numbers' in the high street. At this point, as I felt myself developing a selection of nasty medical symptoms, I realised that there was a choice to be made. Should I plough on, in the hope that the queues might subside? Or should I turn back, deferring my personal hell until a later, possibly even more unbearable occasion? I began to get sweaty shoulders. I'd never had sweaty shoulders before – I wasn't even aware that it was possible to get them – and so I convinced myself that progressing any further today might be dangerous.

After returning empty-handed and wet-shirted from my ring road adventure, I decided to reward myself with a session of my favourite pastime. If I hadn't gone into sales, and more recently the hotel industry, I would almost certainly have put myself forward as a possible secret agent instead. I'm not ashamed of this, but I absolutely love spying on people. I get a real kick out of knowing the ins and outs of the local neighbourhood, and it's fair to say that after years of monitoring I could probably write a series of books on this street alone. I've known about secret affairs for months before the cuckolded husband found out. I've watched an entire police stakeout, back in the days when we had an Italian counterfeiter living across the road (I was practically an honorary member of the team with all the coffee I provided). I've seen boyfriends move in, sofas move out, and even one instance of an exploding barbecue. The view from my living room window has brought me so many cherished moments.

Due to my intensive surveillance, I've got most of the people living around here pinned down. Bloke across the road: chef, two children, ex-wife, new girlfriend, another woman who appears sporadically and is probably his sister. Family to the left: Geoff and co., suit job, hideous taste, lots of arguments, lots of visits to France (possibly a timeshare there). But there's one bunch that I've never really managed to get to grips with. The Street family has lived here, albeit in decreasing numbers, for the best part of five years. On our right-hand side for all of that time, a household has existed in which there have been virtually no incidents of note. Even I, with my KGB-style surveillance skills, have been able to determine virtually nothing of interest about them. There's no shouting, no scandal, no intrigue. It's almost as if they're a normal, happy family – a scenario I could almost believe to be possible if I didn't know better.

That's not to say I know nothing about them: he's a chap of about my age, slightly stockier than I – possibly a rugby player. She's a lady of perhaps three years his junior, pretty, slim, delicate – possibly not a rugby player. They have a son, about the same age as Bianca . . . who, come to think of it, is in her class at school. Hold that thought David – this could be your way in.

Anyway, I mention this uneventful – and therefore I reckon suspicious – household for this reason. I noticed that, as I got out of the Streetmobile after my aborted shopping trip this lunchtime, my mysterious neighbours were also arriving home. Seeing my chance to start our long-overdue first conversation, I scanned the three of them as they stepped out onto the pavement. I was looking for shopping bags, thinking that if they weren't carrying any, they must have fallen victim to the curse of the gridlocked ring road, just like me. As I suspected, there were no bags. I decided to seize the moment.

'Afternoon,' I chirped as cheerfully as possible, fully aware that they probably know me as 'that bloke next door who shouts a lot'.

'Good afternoon,' replied Rugby Man, slightly unnerved by my unexpected verbal ice pick.

'Roads are terrible today, aren't they?' I offered, edging slightly but not quite towards him, a bit like an old crab.

'Looks like it,' he observed, giving away his not-from-round-here accent. Then he dried up a bit and looked at his car, which is almost as rubbish as mine. I took this as my cue to drive the conversation forward.

'I think I might have to do my [swear word] Christmas shopping in the week. Sunday seems to be the new [swear word] Saturday.' I know there was a child present, but I don't think I've explained how [swear word] angry my failed trip made me. 'How far did you get before you decided to turn round then?'

'Actually we were at church,' replied Rugby Man's wife, although she was probably thinking 'This heathen will burn in the fires of hell for eternity.'

'Oh right,' I said, ready to sell the devil my soul providing that he promised to take me now.

'See you around then,' she said, after looking at her husband for a while, and without a trace of irony.

And so they disappeared, leaving me as red-faced as a fat man who's just run the marathon. I found a shred of comfort in the fact that I knew a little more about them, and a good explanation for why they were so oddly quiet. But that was completely overshadowed by the realisation that from now on I would be known to their family as 'That bloke next door who swears a lot'.

Not a good day at all. Not because Hector Malone somehow found inspiration at our breakfast table and wrote another truly awful Christmas card poem on a paper napkin. Not just because Louisa left another patronising answering machine message about 'festive spirit'. Not even because behind door eight on my talking celebrity advent calendar, I found a message from that bloke who gets millions of pounds for presenting clips of animals falling over. No. Today was bad because this evening Bianca and I engaged in a quite enormous argument.

It all started when, fascinated and still slightly embarrassed by the events of yesterday lunchtime, I decided to ask my daughter about the family next door. I started subtly enough, with a few questions about the kids in her class, and whether any of her friends lived very locally. That sort of careful probing produced no dividends though, and so I switched to a more direct approach. To summarise, my main points involved the words 'nutters', 'weirdos' and 'Bible-bashers', while her reply was more along the lines of 'You are a really horrible, negative person who doesn't have any friends.'

Then we really got down to business. I pointed out – quite rightly I feel – that it was hard to be positive in December, when it's cold and everybody wants your money. She came back with a couple of lines about having 'a normal Christmas like everyone else' and not wanting it 'to be like last year'.

So I said, 'Why don't you go and spend Christmas with your mother then?'

To which she replied, 'Maybe I will then.' Which, I have to admit, I wasn't expecting, and represented a very clever manoeuvre for a 13-year-old. She'd called my bluff. So I tried to call hers.

'Fine then. It's settled – I'll call and tell her now.'

At which point Bianca burst into tears and left the building. And then her father punched the fridge.

And that explains why I'm now writing this, with my one remaining hand, in the waiting room of the local Accident and Emergency department. Ah. The doctor will see me now.

It's hard to make beds when you've got one hand in plaster. It's harder to convince your assistant manager to help when she isn't speaking to you and refuses to acknowledge your presence in a room. Thus, as a last, painful resort, I've taken to implementing a discount scheme for guests who do their own chores. So far, the response has been heart-warmingly positive. Hector Malone is even doing the washing up – although it'll take more than that to make me forgive him for his despicable poetry writing.

Being one-handed has more drawbacks than you might first think. You can't play golf, open heavy sash windows, ride a bike or go clay-pigeon shooting. Admittedly, I never do any of those things anyway, but that's hardly the point. There are plenty of things in life which one takes for granted and which suddenly become impossible in the absence of a full compliment of working limbs. Driving is perhaps the most pertinent example, and this proves something of a problem when you are required to make a big scary trip into town.

This morning I found myself with a difficult dilemma. The long-discussed Christmas shopping trip was now somewhat overdue. My plan to avoid the crowds had backfired hideously, and the television was beginning to do those 'only x shopping days till Christmas' announcements. A quiet voice at the back of my mind had begun to gently suggest that I should avoid shopping altogether and give Bianca something home-made, but the memory of her response to last year's Mr Onion-head doll soon told it to be silent. With our relationship fraying severely at the edges, I knew that I didn't truly have a choice about whether to go. But there was still the question of when. Should I give my hand a couple of weeks to heal, and risk the doomsday scenario of shopping on the 24th? Or should I do something even more unthinkable, and brave public transport?

I found myself wedged between a very tall man's armpit and a seated pensioner's wig. The bus journey was only a few minutes long, but in that time I caught a glimpse of what hell might be like. If we'd hit traffic at any point, it's very likely that I would have tried to hold my breath until my head exploded. But somehow, unlike the last time I fatefully attempted to pass down it, the road was virtually clear. That, I soon realised, was because everybody in the world was already in town.

The bus emptied its crowded load onto the high street in a fluid, oozing movement. There we joined another, much larger crowd – a river of work-avoidant people ebbing and flowing past the glitzy windows of a hundred identical storefronts. I barely caught my breath as the crazed hordes – a million people or more loaded up donkey-like with a billion boutique bags – urged me forwards or threatened to trample me under their unmatchable bulk. Somehow I found myself in a packed toy store – a Satan's grotto of grotesque toys all competing to be the number one must-have. 'Pick me!' screamed a nine-inch plastic wrestler who, according to his packaging, can spit authentic looking blood. 'Take me home!' shouted a cuddly doll named 'Bertha the Witch'. At the front of the shop a giant queue did it's best anaconda impression and placed me fifty winding yards from the spotty teenager on the single till. Sighing, I decided to try somewhere else.

The next shop was similarly uninspiring. In here the queue was only half as long, and there were two spotty teenagers instead of one, but when I finally reached them and asked for the Nagatoshi Gamemaster that would act as my passport out of Death Valley, I received a bone-shuddering response.

'Sorry sir, we've sold out of those.'

The same answer was procured from the acne-ridden faces of no fewer than ten further shop assistants. By the time I'd reached the last toy/electronics/department store in town, I was practically crawling on my face.

It had got late. Town was only half full now, and although my mission had once again proved a failure, at least there was some respite to be found in the seat I might get on the bus home. Or so I thought. For town had not emptied itself at all – it's population had simply shifted en masse to the small patch of grass behind the main bus terminus. There were literally thousands of people waiting there to vacuum-pack themselves into the pathetic single-deckers that set off four times an hour. At this rate I would be home some time tomorrow afternoon.

I started to sink to my knees. My left arm began to twinge a little. Perhaps I was going to die here.

And then I saw him. Distant at first, but striding towards me with purpose. A figure in a long coat, with broad shoulders that bore the weight of numerous shopping bags. I couldn't make him out properly – the sun was in its last throes of the day and had decided, for a laugh, to temporarily blind me before setting – but I recognised him, and I proclaimed him my saviour as he spoke the words that freed me from my chains.

'I've got the car,' said Rugby Man. 'Do you want a lift back?'

Wednesday
10th December

During this month of madness, some light relief can always be found in the television guide. Not because it's the key to a fortnight of top-notch family entertainment, of course, but because it swings wide the gate to Room 101 and unleashes a string of everything that's ghastly about that little Pandora's box in the corner of my front room. Watching some of these programmes is a torture akin to having your eyelids pulled off by a tortoise, but reading about them in a poor quality magazine, given away free with *The Daily Strange*, is actually quite fun. This morning, as an even more distant Bianca decided to underline my uselessness by cooking breakfast before school, its arrival on my doormat filled me with the only cheer I'm likely to feel before January.

This year's offering does not disappoint. Witness one channel's effort at impressing on the big day itself – here's prime time viewing on December 25th:

3.10   FILM Braincrusher Saves Christmas 3
John Van Schwarzkof, Ellie Trumper.
Hit family action comedy sequel starring
Schwarzkof as an undercover CIA man who
poses as Santa to infiltrate an international gang
of drug-smuggling elves. Again.
Strange Rating: Three Stars

4.45   Eyes Down Christmas Special
Festive edition of the popular Bingo game show
presented by two fat ladies. Note: in this
edition, the number 22 will be referred to as
'two little turkeys'.

5.30   Give It a Rest Love!
Timeless Christmas 1963 edition of wonder-
fully non-PC comedy, starring Reg Buttsgrove.
Ernie throws bricks at the local corner shop.
(B/W)

6.00   FILM Almost a Tragedy
Billy Breaker, Andrea Andrews.
This is it – the big Christmas blockbuster. Sit
back and enjoy $250 million of mind-blowing
special effects, as John Dollar flawlessly recre-
ates the famous 'North Sea Miss' of 1928, when
two huge ocean liners nearly collided, but
didn't quite.
Strange Rating: Five Stars

8.20   News and Weather.

8.30   Bob's Christmas Surprises
Edited highlights of this morning's live show,
where Bob Sidepart interrupted church services
across the country to play practical jokes, and to
perform a selection of his hits. Caution: may
include vulgar language and some nudity.

9.00   Pie & Mash
They're back again – even though those lovable
cockney rogues were killed off in a huge gas
explosion last Christmas, public demand has
forced them back from the dead for one last
outing. In this feature-length special Tony and
Bill attempt to sell a fake 'shroud of Christ' to
the Pope – with hilarious results!

10.00   Banged Up
This reality show is fast turning into a classic.
Today, we'll watch as the seven remaining
inmates learn that they won't be let out for
Christmas after all, and then discover that one
of them is actually a convicted psychopath.

11.00   Alternative Christmas Thought
With Gary Smarm, chairman of the Smarm
Shopping Mall Group.

11.15   Guy Bongo – Up the Front
A special recording of Bongo's recent
North-of-England pub and club tour. Inspira-
tional.

12.30 FILM Son of God
Gregory Joseph, Maria Muldoon.
Multi-award-winning biopic. Dull.
Strange Rating: One Star.

2.15 FILM Whoops – Wrong Jesus!
Eric Parp, Julie Trousers.
Classic bawdy Bible farce – such a shame it's on
so late. Set the video for this one.
Strange Rating: Five Stars.

How I chuckle as I think of the millions of
morons who'll gobble up that diet of junk-food
TV so ravenously. This is supposedly the very
best that television has to offer – a clutch of
out-of-date movies, a sitcom that's evolving
from 'classic' into 'overcooked', a couple of
game shows, a couple of repeats, and for no
good reason, a feature-length pop concert from
a bloke with a ridiculous name. Quite
co-incidentally – or perhaps not – Mr Bongo's
voice was to be found behind door 10 on my
advent calendar this morning. He told me to
'watch out' for his Christmas special, which I
will. Just as I 'watch out' for speeding buses
when I'm crossing the street.

I wouldn't say that Rugby Man and I are quite
friends yet – clearly I still don't even know his
real name – but I wouldn't rule such a develop-
ment out in the future. From our conversation in
his car yesterday, I've gathered that he is not only

kind and compassionate (he spotted me on my knees yesterday; I hadn't seen him; he could have just walked by) but also forgiving and genuine. No mention was made of my four-letter outburst in front of his children. Instead, he asked me about my business, about my daughter, and about me. That's the most interest that anyone's shown in my life since our last visit from the taxman. So despite the fact that I know virtually nothing about him (with all those questions pointing in my direction, there was no time to send any back his way), he's already become my favourite neighbour. And, perhaps far more surprisingly, I think he quite likes me too.

By the look of things, that view is mirrored in our respective offspring. Through the top flap of the bathroom window (which offers the best view of Rugby Man's backyard), I watched this afternoon as Bianca spent a full hour talking with Rugby Man Junior. They may even have talked for longer than that: my surveillance operation ended suddenly when Hector Malone burst in to find me standing on the toilet and I nearly broke another limb; I didn't see Bianca for at least another hour.

When she did return, I made a valiant attempt at patching up our strained relationship. I figured that the best way to do this would be to find some common ground:

'The family next door seems very nice,' I offered, with a big beaming smile and a plate of biscuits in my good hand. (This usually works very well with dogs, although I'd never tried it on a teenager before.)

She folded her arms and huffed. This was not the best-case-scenario response, but I persisted anyway:

'Their son's in your class isn't he?'

'What are you going to say?' she asked, her voice half angry, half tired.

'What do you mean? I just think they seem like nice people.'

'That's not what you think. That's never what you think. You never think anyone seems nice.'

This wasn't going very well. Any moment now she was going to whip out the line about me having no friends.

'Most people aren't very nice,' I retaliated, stupidly.

'This is why you don't have any friends' she said. (See!)

That hurt, even though I knew it was coming, and it knocked the wind out of me. She started to edge away from me, perhaps feeling a little bit guilty. I tried one more time:

'I do like them. Honestly. I've been chatting to . . . er . . . him the last couple of days. He's a nice bloke.'

'Jimmy says you swore at his parents.'

'No I didn't!' I gasped, before remembering. 'Well, yes I did – but not at them! Just while they were standing there. I was angry about the traffic.'

Bianca stood speechless for a while, giving me the sort of look she gave when I once explained why sometimes it was alright for Daddy to lie. Then she laughed a bit, and edged back towards me. Some of the frostiness thawed, and she even took a biscuit. I wonder whether other dog training tricks transfer to the practice of daughter-raising.

'I can't believe you swore at Jimmy's parents! They go to church and everything!' She was giggling uncontrollably now.

'I don't think they were too bothered,' I explained. 'His dad gave me a lift back from town yesterday and he didn't even mention it. I think we're going to be friends.'

Bianca very nearly spat out her mouthful of biscuit. I took from this that she was surprised, and that therefore she sees me as a bit of a loner. We chatted for a while about school, and the weather for a while after that, but I couldn't get her response out of my mind.

I'm not old enough to be a sad old loner. Tomorrow I'm going to make a new friend. Maybe even a new best friend.

Thursday
11th December

As I've mentioned already, Christmas Day three years ago was the worst day of my life. It involved no joy, no cheer, no fun, and no family togetherness. In fact, it consisted of quite the opposite. My wife and I woke up arguing, having gone to sleep arguing the night before. When the sun rose, and before little Bianca had even had a chance to make her annual scamper to the foot of our bed, we wheeled out the heavy artillery and began to shoot down the curtain on a marriage which once, long, long ago, had never seemed destined for such an end.

We went for each other like two rabid animals. I called her names I didn't think I'd ever utter; she assassinated my character like a well-trained sniper. The conflict literally lasted for the whole day: in the morning we opened presents from each other and childishly destroyed them; at lunchtime we substituted cracker jokes for insults and spat out the things that the other one had cooked; in the evening we watched terrible television and argued over what to watch even though we knew we'd hate everything on every channel. It was a day of total darkness, without even a shimmer of light. A day of hatred, bereft of a single caring glance. And at the end of it, with our throats aching and our dignity laid bare on the wood-laminate flooring, we floated over some invisible red line and found ourselves in the place we always swore we'd never reach.

She'd said some pretty ugly things about me. Called me a pessimist, a miser, a defeatist, a loser, an antisocial underachiever. And she gave me this one terrible, unrepeatable look. Only once, and right at the end. It was a look that cut right through me in a second and left my head rolling around on the floor. I'll never forget that look, because it said all this in a glance: 'I loved you once David, and put you on a pedestal. And now I don't love you any more, and you'll never matter to me ever again.'

So after that look, and all the words that encased it, I wanted nothing more than for her to walk out of the door and never come back. And that's what she did, though where she found a place to stay at that time on Christmas evening I still don't know, and probably never will.

I'm still not quite sure why things came to a head in such a way, and on that day of all days. Part of it was because I'd just lost my job, and because we'd only just rubber-stamped the biggest investment of our lives. And part of it was because we never fixed any of the things that we argued about in all the other fights. It also had a little to do with my penchant for negativity, and a little to do with her love of spending money and living the high life. But it wasn't because of the time of year. It wasn't because it was Christmas. It seems strange to say it now, but I used to actually quite like Christmas.

I mention that because this evening I explained it all to someone else for the first time in a very long while. As promised, I paid a visit – with bottom-of-the-range bottle of wine in hand – to Mark, the well-built neighbour previously known as Rugby Man/Jimmy's dad. Despite the fact that I had apparently interrupted a cosy family evening, Mark invited me to stay, ushered his wife and children out of the front room, and sat me in his best chair. Then he cracked open the wine, poured two glasses, and began to engage me in friendly conversation.

'So –' he began, a little puzzled by my visit. 'How's your hand?' Which was again an example of his caring and compassionate nature. I like him. I want to be his friend. So I said:

'Still broken, but at least it isn't the one I use for arm wrestling.' Why on earth did I say that?

'Oh really?' he chuckled. 'So you're still a champion with the good one?'

Clearly I am not. Clearly this line of conversation was taking me towards a violent sporting struggle with my well-built Christian neighbour. Clearly I am a complete idiot. So I said:

'You bet!'

And there we were. Elbows on the coffee table, hands clasped together, watched by a thirteen-year-old referee who I was sure could be relied upon to relate this story back to my daughter within minutes. Now I don't like to admit this, but both Louisa and Bianca were making valid points when, at repeated intervals over the last five years, they accused me of being friendless. Truth is, I've never been surrounded by people I could count on and be there for, and that's mainly because of my incredible ability to make abysmal first impressions. Another classic example was now in progress.

'Ready?' Clearly young Jimmy was relishing this, having often watched his father rip people's arms off on the sports field.

We both nodded. Little beads of sweat, which might as well have been labelled in pink neon with the word 'Pansy', began to appear and trickle all over my tensed-up face.

Then we began. We both stared intensely at the other, with gritted teeth and bulging arms. For just a few moments, this contest meant more than life itself. If I could just start well, and fend off his early pressure, perhaps I could give a good account of myself. Perhaps it wouldn't be an embarrassment – at the end he might tap me on the shoulder and say 'Whoa – that was a close one.'

It was he who struck first, pushing with all his might against my previously unreckoned strength. I refused to relent. Instead I cranked up the power in my arm, and watched as my opponent baulked a little. I saw my chance – I'd caught him off guard and was now in the position to complete the surprise. Focusing every ounce of energy in my body, every drop of blood in my veins, and all my mental toughness into that one bicep, I began to drive him back, further and further, degree by degree. After a good minute's struggle, I had his hand an inch from the table, and although he was still resisting gamely, we both knew that the battle was won. Suddenly, the world went into freeze-frame. I glanced at young Jimmy, almost in tears at the prospect of seeing me beat the Goliath to whom he had always looked up. Then I eyeballed the once-great man, dripping with sweat and with his defiance sapping away, and mouthed two words: 'you lose'. Then I brought his hand crashing onto the table, denting it slightly, and leapt up to punch the air. Then someone draped an American flag across my shoulders, and there was a big fanfare.

That's not really what happened. In truth he didn't try for the first five seconds, then suddenly twisted my puny little stick-arm backwards and slammed it onto the table, before letting out an enormous laugh.

This was all very embarrassing. And as Jimmy sneaked out, having not been called upon to make any tight decisions, I knew it was going to get even more embarrassing tomorrow. Still, it was over, and mercifully quickly. I sat back, rubbing my arm with my plaster cast, and took a gulp of the wine. Then I wished that I hadn't, because it tasted like wee.

But after that, something strange happened. Mark grabbed his glass too, and took a great swig of the contents. As it reacted with his taste buds, he let out a little squeak of surprise. He didn't spit into a bucket, but it was pretty obvious that was what he wanted to do. The bottle had been a gift, and I could tell that he didn't want to offend me. But I could also tell that he would rather kiss a recently-fed dog than take in any more. So instead of coughing and complaining, he just retracted into his chair and went a bit purple. With my hand and arm still smarting, I was amused by the plate of revenge which my cheapskate off-licence choice had served up. So then, just as Mark had a few moments earlier, I descended into sniggering.

Mark looked up, his mouth still smarting from the assault launched on it by this unusual booze. His smile had quickly faded, but seeing my reaction brought it back, and soon we were both laughing out loud. We continued to do so for a concerning amount of time – a casual observer would have imagined either that the air was full of dentist's gas, or else that we both needed certifying. Obviously, one of the contributing factors to this debacle was the arm wrestle – the manner of my defeat; the fact that we'd done it in the first place. And another was the presence in the middle of the table of the worst bottle of wine on God's earth. There was one more factor though – something much harder to define but undeniably present in the air. In the most bizarre way, we'd relaxed into each other's company. Despite what seemed like an awful start – a four-letter outburst, hand-to-hand combat and bad wine – it felt like we were friends. And so we laughed, because of what had gone on, but also because we were enjoying ourselves.

'Where on earth did you get that wine?' asked Mark after composing himself.

'From the Mini-mart. I'm so sorry – I had no idea what it would taste like. It had a nice picture on the bottle.' I make no secret of being an ignoramus with wines.

'It's certainly different. I've never tried Ghanaian wine before. Perhaps it's not geared to the western palate.'

'Mark, I cannot believe we had an arm wrestle in your front room. You must think I'm a complete weirdo.'

'Why? I didn't mind. It was good fun. Why can't two friends have some fun in the evening when they've worked hard all day?'

I ignored what he said about working hard all day and concentrated on the first part of the sentence. I wondered about what to say next, and it's a good job that Mark bounded in before I could say anything, as I was getting a bit confused and was about to ask if he'd like to go to the pictures tomorrow night. It really has been a long time since I've had a friend.

'So David, tell me something,' he started, leaning in towards me. 'My wife and I have always noticed that you don't seem to like Christmas. You don't do decorations, you don't give out cards. I hope you don't think I spy on people (if only he knew), but I've never even seen you with a Christmas tree. Have I got this all wrong, or have you got a problem with this time of year?'

And so I told him everything that I just told you. And I told him other things too, about Louisa, Bianca and me, about my house guests, my friends (who I had to invent on the spot), and more. I'm sure I'll fill you in on the rest sometime soon, but it's getting late now, and tomorrow night I'm supposed to be going to the pictures with Mark.

The house is over-half full at the moment, and to-morrow, as three young farmers (!) come to town for some kind of festive jolly, we'll reach capacity for the first time since July's tourist rush, when a woman in the next street found a tomato with the face of the Madonna on it. If you remember, Hector Malone was first in, and has steadily descended since from being one of my favourite guests ever, to being quite the opposite. At first I found him witty, intelligent, classy and mysterious. Now I see that it's all a front, behind which lies the worst, most soulless poetry-writing mind the world has ever seen. An easy mistake to make, I'm sure you'll understand.

After Hector, we were joined by a group with whom I've had hardly any dealings so far. Three doctors, or at least, three men who have the prefix 'Dr' attached to their names, arrived when I wasn't looking and have managed to almost completely avoid me ever since. Apparently Bianca's been looking after them, and since they continue to pay their way I can only assume that she's doing a good job.

Actually, I'm sure that Bianca has been doing a good job. She'll certainly be doing it better than her father would. She may only be thirteen, but she can already cook better than me, clean better than me, and – goes without saying really – is much better with the whole public relations side of the operation. I'm feeling quite redundant as a result, which is quite ironic actually, considering that it's Christmas.

I used to be quite a little hotshot. Working in sales is a cut-throat business: you either make your target and earn your commission, or else you walk the plank like all the other not-quite-good-enoughs. Back when I worked for J P Truelove Associates I was one of the best target-makers they'd ever seen. You might be quite surprised, if tacky Christmas novelties can feel surprise, to hear that I excelled in a role which, let's face it, involves communicating with other human beings. But in fact, my lack of social skills made it a lot easier for me. I loved it – and what's more I was really good at it too. I was fast; I didn't get bogged down in asking people how they were or how their cat was; I drove home the sale. Some might have called me abrupt, intimidating, even rude, but I didn't care. Other salespeople would beg me for my secrets, such was my unattainable superiority at the summit of the team rankings. I was a sales superstar. But then, unfortunately, a few people did call me abrupt, intimidating, and especially rude, and I was made to care. On Christmas Eve, the day before the worst Christmas ever, I lost my job because an 'important client' demanded it. Which is another reason why this time of the year isn't always associated with joy and cheer in the David Street psyche.

Had 'fun' this evening. It was a strange experience, the kind of which, outside of the context of my relationship with Bianca, I haven't had in a very long time. She and I have been doing pizza and video evenings since before time began, but a pizza and cinema trip is a rarity indeed. And in a complete break from the norm, that's exactly what we embarked upon this evening, flanked by Mark and his son, an apparent arm-wrestling referee turned movie buff.

'We should see the new Van Schwarzkof film,' he said with authority as we stood in line at the box office, our bellies full of very good, non-delivery pizza (a true delicacy for the Streets). 'It's supposed to be an action comedy with a series of twists. I've read very good things about it.' He suddenly sounded a bit like the film review guy from TV, who was behind door 9 of my talking advent calendar a couple of days ago, and said 'I'd give your Christmas tree a five star rating' (which would have been much more effective if we'd had one). He also sounded a bit too clever and precocious for a thirteen-year-old, and I felt my well-documented irritability rising up inside.

'Perhaps we'll let David and Bianca decide this time,' offered Mark quickly. 'Anything take your fancy?' I added 'generous of spirit' to my growing list of Mark plus-points. This seeing-the-good-in-people game is a cinch.

'I'm not too bothered to be honest Mark . . . ' I said feebly. 'Why don't you choose.'

'I've got one!' shrieked Bianca.

My eyes flashed across to the line up of posters on the cinema wall. Which one could have interested her so much as to force that kind of sound out of her? *Splatfest 6: Return of the Cleaver*? Possibly, but surely not in the presence of churchgoing folk. *Fluffy Bunny goes to Snuggletown*? Perhaps, if she was still four. I couldn't see a movie that she would like – I was sure of it. But then, suddenly, it dawned on me, a millisecond too late to dive full-length towards her and cup my plaster cast over her mouth. How could she do this to me?

'How about *A Very Merry Christmas*?'

Jimmy, bless him, helpfully informed us that this was a romantic comedy of some repute, and agreed with the critics that it might be quite good.

Mark said, 'That's settled then,' and I tried to swallow my tongue.

But actually – and I can't quite believe that I'm writing this at all, let alone on the pages of a

'Christmas Diary' – it wasn't too bad. Obviously it was a hideously soppy romance, the kind of which makes a failed husband's skin crawl, but it also had a pretty commendable message. If we all still had a grasp of that old idea 'It's better to give than to receive'; if we were all still more interested in spending time with those closest to us than erecting dancing Santa robots; if we still attached some kind of meaning to Christmas, apart from commercialism and loneliness. . . . Well, then maybe, like the characters in this and so many other works of fiction, we'd have something.

As it is, we have nothing. Nothing except a very expensive, very uncomfortable day, with very bad television. Ha. Bet you thought I was making progress then.

Saturday
13th December

The 13th of the month and, fittingly, I receive another message from Hades. The phone rings, about midday, and since I can see that my only friend is in his garden, and the only other person I care about is showing three very odd-looking teenagers to their lodgings, I ignore it. But I listen to the message:

> 'David, it's me. I think we need to talk. Come on David, pick up the phone. I want to talk to you. We can't have another Christmas like this. Pick up the phone David.'

Listening to your ex-wife, whom you hate, pleading with you repeatedly to talk to her is a bit like listening to a child scratch his nails down a blackboard. It's excruciating. But when your only usual communication is made through legal channels, answering machine messages and doorstep gifts, it's better to sit and listen in agony than to do the unthinkable and actually speak to her.

'David, I'm sorry about the present I left on your doorstep. It was a bad joke. I wish I hadn't put it there. Please pick up the phone. DAVID!' Beep.

With that last yelp, she hung up. But the note on which she departed, and which remained, pendulous in the air, was chilling and unusual. There was a desperation in her voice that she'd never allowed to creep into one of her messages before. For a moment I was worried about her. For a moment I even considered calling her back. But something interrupted me, and I let her slip my mind.

But now I've remembered again. And I can still hear that change in her voice. Not sure what to think about that really.

Sunday
14th December

I was woken early by the most horrendous noise. A huge white truck with 'Blando Stores' emblazoned on the side was pulling up directly outside. I grabbed the first piece of clothing I could find – an old dressing gown – and ran to the front window, just in time to see a giant, bearded man in a red felt costume leaping from the cab. Unlike any Santa I've seen before, this chap was carrying a large clipboard, and had a pencil behind one ear. Perhaps times had become harder in Lapland, and its citizens now had to work for more than one evening a year.

Santa had brought a delivery for Geoff, my second-favourite next-door neighbour. A large delivery. In fact so large that, on the big man's command, an elf had to jump out of the back of the truck to help with the unloading. Bag after bag, box after box came scurrying past my window on elf-legs. It's no understatement to say that a several ton vehicle was being emptied before my eyes.

I strained to see if I could spot anything

specific in this bulk of packaged objects. But perhaps I strained too hard.

'Hello David!' cooed cheery old Geoff. 'Come on out and have a look!'

I was so pleased.

'Hello Geoff.' I said, desperately trying to force some enthusiasm into my voice. 'You're putting on quite a show this morning.'

'Look who's talking,' cracked Geoff, indicating my attire, which, unfortunately, turned out to be Bianca's dressing gown, and not mine after all.

The two deliverymen both guffawed at this point, which, considering that they were dressed up as Santa and his elf, was a bit like having a fireball lobbed at you by two people sheltering in an igloo. I ignored them though, and pulled the pink 'Dozy Dog' gown tight in the appropriate places.

'My one's in the wash,' I attempted, and all three of them looked at the floor with motor-way-width smirks on their faces.

Eventually, after Geoff had signed for his delivery, and the reindeer riders had returned to their truck for a mince pie and a sherry, I got some sense out of him. 'You know David,' he began, 'that what I have here on this lawn is everything I need for a happy Christmas this year.'

I looked across at the eight-foot dancing puppet attached to the side of Geoff's place, and

thought long and hard about differing defini-
tions of the word 'need'. Then I nodded in a very
uncommitted manner. He continued:

'And what's more, I didn't even have to leave
my house. In fact, I didn't even have to leave my
chair. Did it all in one place, on the Internet. I can
see you're impressed.'

I was impressed. The idea that the hell of
shopping could now be avoided through tech-
nology was almost too much. If I actually had a
computer capable of connecting to the Internet,
I'd have been in raptures. Geoff kept on selling
it:

'Food, decorations, crackers, a cheeky bottle
of drink or six! It's all here David, all on this
lawn.'

Silently I prayed for sudden torrential rain.

'And that's not the half of it! In these boxes,
the most important part of all – the presents!
Dolls for little Angie, a new calculator for Uncle
Neville, one of those Nagatoshi Gamemaster
things for Kevin, an inflatable . . . '

'Stop!' I bellowed, almost involuntarily. 'Go
back one.'

'OK David, keep your little dressing gown
on. I said one of those Nagatoshi Gamemaster
things for Kevin.'

Five minutes later (after switching to the
correct dressing gown and picking up a rather
dusty credit card), I was sitting in the last
place on earth I thought I'd ever be: in

Geoff-next-door's study, on a leather swivel chair.

An excited Geoff – somehow I don't figure that he has too many friends either – was fiddling with the computer in front of me. And I was excited too, because fate had presented me with a very palatable possibility indeed. According to Geoff, the Blando Stores website still had a few of these little games consoles available, and were guaranteeing delivery in time for the big day. This was my golden chance to get out of jail free.

'OK,' he grinned after a short while. 'Grab the mouse.'

And I did, although doing so was rather strange and uncomfortable, since I had to use my wrong hand instead of the usual (now broken) one. It was slow, but I'd get there in the end.

Now as I've already suggested, it's unlikely that Geoff and his family often have house guests. He's an intensely irritating human being. Therefore, on one of the rare occasions that someone does cross his threshold, say, to use him for his flashy computer, he tries really hard to impress. Perhaps this explains why, just as I began to navigate the Blando website at sub-catatonic speeds, I was thrown off balance by Geoff's stereo system, which was cranked into full-volume action by it's enthusiastic owner, who thought I might like to hear his latest great CD purchase, entitled *Massive Christmas Hits*.

Having recently got into the swing of fighting with neighbours, that title sounded like quite a good description of what I wanted to give Geoff right then. But I couldn't, because the glittering prize of a great present for my wonderful daughter, was almost in the grip of my wrong hand. So I just grimaced, very obviously, but somehow he took this as an indication of encouragement, and ploughed things on to the next level.

'Cool eh?' asked Geoff annoyingly. 'And check this out!'

Then I went temporarily blind. As my ability to see slowly filtered back, I was confronted by a hideously garish display of super-bright green and red lights, burning into my eyes like lasers from every conceivable angle. Geoff has the outside of his house rigged up with thousands of little bulbs, and I've often made fun, but that's nothing compared to what he has inside.

The room, and the computer screen, which was now displaying 'electrical goods', had turned into a blur – a mash of colours that looked like very bad art. I was so close to my goal, but my ears and eyes were being seriously assaulted. And by Christmas-related assailants too. I felt like a starving pilgrim, sunburnt and blistered but so close to the holy shrine. I pressed on.

Why Geoff believed that anybody would enjoy this horrific combination is beyond me. What's much more staggering is that when he saw me, huddled over his computer with squinty eyes and my dressing gown hood up, he still somehow deduced that we were having fun together. So he called to his children, who understandably thought there was some kind of festive party going on, and ran in dressed in a really poor Rudolph-the-Red-Nosed-Reindeer costume which their mum had clearly made. Probably while very ill.

I was on the 'enter your credit card details' screen, but seeing Rudolph – especially a Rudolph with one antler and stitched up eye-holes – was too much. I bolted from my seat, and made for the door.

Geoff wasn't going to let me go without a fight, and shouted to two-man Rudolph to give chase. So there I was, fleeing a nightmarish room of 9,000 decibel musical cheese and scary alien landing lights, and hotly pursued by two children in a recycled cow costume. I made it through Geoff's front door, and out on to the street (which, of course, was unusually full of locals for ten o'clock on a Sunday morning), then watched as Rudolph seriously debilitated himself by running into the gatepost. His stunned front portion fell to the ground, crying the tears of a little boy, while his hind legs just sort of wandered aimlessly around the garden for a while, a bit lost on their own. I breathed something of a sigh of relief, despite my failure to hold nerve at the final hurdle, and allowed myself a little smile.

Then I saw Mark, and his family, getting in the car to go to church. I waved, and then a sudden gust of wind blew open my dressing gown, and I got bad sense of déjà vu. So after that start to the day, the only option was to return to my bed, and unsurprisingly I've been too terrified to leave it ever since.

Monday
15th December

Too angry to write anything about today. Good-
night.

Tuesday
16th December

Picture the scene if you will. It's Monday morning, and the breakfast room is buzzing like never before. Six of our seven guests have decided to eat at the same time, and my assistant and I are buzzing around the room balancing notepads, plates and toast-racks. The three young farmers are dominating the main table, and show no willingness to budge for anyone. The doctors, being intelligent men, have found an alternative use for the big cupboard in the corner (which is short, wide and deep with a flat top), and have seated themselves, on barstools borrowed from the kitchen, around the three sides of it which aren't pressed against the wall. Every seat, every surface in that room is being taken up, but somehow we're coping. Then I hear the high and hearty pitch of a man returning from his morning exercises, and we have a problem.

'Hullo!' chirps Hector. 'Hope there's room for one more!'

Each of the thuggish-looking youths clustered around the breakfast table spends a moment looking at their trainers, which are perched upon another chair on the other side of the table, then looks back at their cornflakes. The intellectuals look sheepish and give a collective shrug. Hector looks a little stung for a moment, but just then has a flash of inspiration.

'Oh well,' he says, looking at me. 'I'll just have to sit in the kitchen.'

So it's not enough that I have to cook fourteen eggs and half a pig, but I have to do so in the company of a man who epitomises naff. When Hector first checked in to the Streets Ahead Guesthouse, I quite liked him. I was impressed by him even. But since I discovered his profession – chief purveyor of the true mean-inglessness of Christmas – I've liked him less and less. And it's funny how, once you're down on someone, you start to find all sorts of other things that irritate you. Hector wears 'zany' ties for example. I found that endearing at first, now I can barely look at him. Also, he reads *The Daily Spectacle*. I used to see this as a sign of his intel-lectualism, but now I've identified it as a hollow attempt to merely appear intellectual. It's funny how your opinion of someone can so drastically change in such a short space of time.

'So,' says Hector, resting on his elbows at the end of the kitchen worktop. 'Not long to go now. I love Christmas.'

'You came to the wrong house,' I say, tossing the bacon. 'It's the bloke next door you wanted.'

'Yes, I saw all those presents he had delivered. Smart way to do your Christmas shopping – I wish I'd thought of that. Maybe I could ask to use his computer!'

I nod silently as the slightly disturbing image of a home-made reindeer staggers across the theatre of my mind. Hector goes on:

'Still haven't got around to doing my shopping yet. I've left it late I know. Suppose you did yours months ago, did you Mr Street?'

This is a sore point, and makes me spill a sausage.

'No, actually. I've still got one present left to get.'

Bianca huffs, knowing that the only present I ever buy is for her, and goes to check on orange juice refills. With her out of the room, I'm free to explain to Hector – with pent-up venom:

'She wants one of those video game things,' I hiss. 'A Nagatoshi Gamemaster. But I can't find one anywhere. So I'm going to have to buy her something second-rate instead. And that wouldn't matter, if we didn't live in a world where people moan when they get 'the wrong present'. That's what she'll do, if I don't manage to get what she's asked for. Now some people might say that's her problem, but not me. It's not her fault that she's grown up in a world where everyone has always got to have the latest thing. It's not her fault that she's grown up in a place where all that counts is how much money you've got and how much stuff you've bought with it.' I'm nearly shouting now.

'You know, everybody rushes out to buy a Christmas tree, and decorate it with shiny balls and tinsel each year. But no one has a clue about why they're actually doing it. Hector, do you know why people always have to have a Christmas tree? Do you know what it's supposed to represent, or what it adds, or why people have always done it? Because I don't.'

Hector shakes his head, and wishes he hadn't started this. I carry on ranting.

'No. But still your company pumps out these half-baked cards with pictures of trees with shiny balls and tinsel on. And you put poems inside which make people feel a little warm, and gooey, and slightly less guilty about spending shameful amounts of money for one day, as long as they happen to like Christmas. And if they don't like Christmas, if they're part of this silent minority of people like me for whom this time of year completely stinks, well they'll just have to swallow it, like a big stodgy lump of Christmas pudding.'

Hector starts to nervously form the beginnings of a response, but is interrupted by the sound of the letterbox. I go to check, and find a single piece of hand-delivered mail, addressed in silver ink. It's a card, which is unusual, and what's more it's a local card, which is more like a miracle. Ironically, it has a picture of a

Christmas tree, complete with tinsel and shiny balls, on the front. I open it up to see if the hand of H. Malone can be witnessed within, but as I do so a slip of paper, which at first I mistake for a cheque (million-to-one shot territory at the best of times) falls out on the floor. I pick it up, flip it over, and read:

St Mark's Church on the Hill

Mark, Polly, Jimmy and Ruth

Would like to invite

David and Bianca

To our Christmas celebrations

On

Christmas Eve at 11.30 p.m.

And

Christmas Day at 10.00 a.m.

At St Mark's Church, St Mark's Hill

And suddenly a gigantic penny, the size of a large boulder, drops noisily inside my head. Then the smoke alarm in the hall goes crazy, Bianca rushes in to the kitchen to save the breakfast, and I lock myself in the bathroom for the rest of the morning.

Wednesday
17th December

It's been a long time since I've experienced friendship. So long in fact, that I can tell you a lot about the last friend I had. Five and a half years ago, Simon Harris, my closest chum since back in school, took the wise decision to leave this horrible country for a life running a bar in Melbourne, Australia. Simon was the same age as me, and at five feet and ten inches, about an inch shorter than me. Over the decades, we generally copied each other's hair styles, mainly because we always seemed to like the same bands. We both married young, and we both settled in the area in which we had grown up. I had a daughter, he had three sons; he liked travel, I didn't; his marriage fell apart because of adultery, and mine fell apart because my wife was insane. That's pretty much an overview of us, although I should add that he lost his wife three years earlier than me, and his resulting depression sent him thousands of miles away, while mine just led me to go into catering.

I was gutted when he left – even though I understood his decision to do so – and never really met anyone since who matched up. Simon was an unbelievably nice bloke: warm, kind, generous, funny – the lot. I've met a great number of people in the last five years, albeit mainly only for breakfast, and I've never come across a person like him. But this month, I thought I'd found somebody. Somebody to watch sport with, moan about women with, share jokes and whisky and problems with. Someone warm, kind, generous and funny, who was interested in me and my life purely because he was a nice bloke.

But Mark wasn't really what he seemed. He tried to be, or at least, he pretended to be, the friend my doctor has always told me I needed. But in fact, he was only trying to be nice so he could get my defences down and invite me to church.

So all this was 'evangelism'? The lift home, the arm wrestle, the cosy buddy trip to the cinema and pizza place? All of it was warm up work as he got ready to ask politely for my soul? Christmas may be a cynical time these days, but this is taking the biscuit. I feel sick just thinking about it.

So this is lined up to be a great Christmas. I have a broken hand, I still haven't done any Christmas shopping, the friend count is back down to zero, and most of the neighbourhood has seen me fleeing in panic from two children in a pantomime costume. And, my ex-wife has restarted her answering machine message terror campaign (another short example today). I thought I might have seen the end of that when she quietened down about six months ago.

'David, give me a call. Please. How long are you going to keep this up?' Beep.

If I could go and hide in a wardrobe for the next week and a half, I would.

I've tried not to moan about my hand, but it's really starting to irritate me now. Not just because the skin under the plaster is so itchy – but also because so many daily tasks, my proficiency at which I've always taken for granted, have suddenly become either much more difficult or completely impossible. I can't drive, I can't swim, I can't make use of that cobwebbed gym membership which I've just remembered about. I now have to toss bacon like a pancake, instead of flipping it with a spatula. I now have to put my beer can down before reaching for the remote control. Room cleaning is an ordeal, simple objects like telephones and ironing boards have become instruments of torture and enforced contortion. And don't even let me get started on personal hygiene. I never knew how much I liked having two hands, or how much I'd miss one when it was gone. Why did it have to happen at this time of year?

You've hardly succeeded in your mission to 'help me to help myself' in 'rediscovering the reason for the season', but you've certainly been useful for cataloguing some very good examples of why that mission was always quite impossible. Hector Malone, with his soulless ditties, is a great example. Geoff next door, with his lights, sounds and demented children, is another. In fact you, and particularly the nauseating gift set that accompanies you, are another big indicator. You see, I've always thought, and this year I've just had my views confirmed, that the true meaning of Christmas these days is that it's all about meaninglessness. People make money out of it, people revel in and celebrate it, and people use it as an excuse to burst shirt buttons and buy new belts, but no one really has a clue why. And if anyone really asked that question – I mean anybody significant, like politicians, newspapermen, wacktastic TV presenters – the sad truth is that very few people would have an answer, and we'd all have to turn our thoughts to Easter . . . although don't get me started on that.

Mark is a slightly different case of course – he obviously thinks that there is some kind of meaning buried under all the left-over turkey. I don't have a problem with that per se, but I do object to forming part of some ripe-and-ready mission field for him and his church buddies to plough. And as for all this baby-in-a-manger stuff: I mean, it's great for the kids and all that, but can't we just admit that it's something you grow out of when you reach adulthood? It's never hurt Santa's popularity, has it? Perhaps I'll make this point to Mark when I explain why we're no longer friends.

Anyway, I suppose what I'm saying is that I've quite enjoyed having you around after all. You haven't made me feel any better about Christmas; in fact if anything, writing it all down just makes my feelings clearer. But you have been a fun distraction, and the only friend to have lasted more than two weeks.

Which is more than I can say about the other bits of tat which you arrived with. I noticed, when I found you on my doorstep at the start of the month, that you were sitting on top of, and not inside the box containing the talking advent calendar and 'Ten Things to Make Your Christmas Great' list – now I've realised that you were deliberately distancing yourself from them. I can't blame you. Door 18 on the calendar revealed yet another advert, this time for running shoes. 'Get a pair before they run out' joked a robot. Now I'll take my hat off to whoever wrote that gag – clearly they're a cut above mere mortals like our Hector – but the fact is that this morning's offering had absolutely nothing to do with Christmas. It didn't even try, half-heartedly, to appear festive. Instead of the usual picture of Holly, Ivy or the MD of Magico™ in a Santa hat, there was a shoe. It seems (and I know now that it doesn't get any better, having ripped open doors 19–24) that either the people at Magico™ ran out of C-list celebrities too early, or that they decided to sell off the final doors to the highest bidder. From what I can see, the C-list is pretty long. I'll go for the latter. The talking advent calendar is thus no more.

Having disposed of offending item number one, I turned my thoughts to the crumpled piece of paper which still lay untouched on my bedroom floor. I'd never read more than the title before, but had gathered from it that this would be a catalogue of things that could make my Christmas 'merrier'. I'd assumed, quite naturally I think, to find the clichéd old list of songs, food, decorations and family arguments. But I had once again overestimated those wonderful little elves at Magico™. In fact, the list consists of ten must-have products which I 'really should buy' to 'show them I care'. Fighting toys, talking electronic personal organiser, cheese making set. The crumpled piece of paper has joined the talking advent calendar in the bin.

So you, my friend, are all that's left of the Magico™ 'True Meaning of Christmas Gift Set'. And all I'm left wondering is whether you are waiting to betray me like all the rest. Will there be an advert for health-improving magnetic jewellery or solar-powered food mixers on one of your final pages? Please don't let me down.

Friday
19th December

My daughter is thirteen. She is still a child. It'll be years yet before the law rates her a viable drinker, gambler, or driver. Thirteen, for pity's sake.

I was enraged. I caught my reflection in the hallway mirror as I stormed out of the house, and noticed that I'd turned into a giant tomato. I didn't care – I was going to give that meathead next door a piece of my mind.

I made three small dents in the wood of Mark's front door as I battered it with my plaster cast. The man himself arrived almost instantly, and his unimpressed face fell further when he realised from my redness that I was unlikely to be accepting his little invitation.

'Can you not keep your children under control?' I bellowed.

Mark looked stunned. Clearly he was unaware of little Jimmy's crime.

'I beg your pardon mate?' he tried.

'Don't you "mate" me,' I yelled. 'I've just found your son taking advantage of my Bianca.'

Then, incredibly, he gave a little laugh. If he wasn't much bigger and stronger than me, I would have knocked him out just for that, the patronising idiot.

'Yes, I've noticed they've been getting closer,' he said calmly.

'You mean you're happy about this? Your child is running around behaving like Don Juan de Marco and you're happy about it?'

'It's one girl, who he really seems to like. And they're both thirteen. They're not children anymore David.'

'Yes they are! They're barely out of nappies. Anyway matey, you didn't see them. I caught them.'

'Caught them doing what?'

'Well he was . . . you know, kissing her. Properly.'

'I think you should be pretty thankful if that's the worst your kid is up to at thirteen.'

His inability to become ruffled, or to seem to care in the slightest about this situation, was helping me to evolve from a boiling tomato to a blistering beetroot. Then, once again, the penny dropped.

'Hang on,' I said, 'I know what this is all about.'

'All what David?'

'You're trying to get her on side, like you did with me.'

'What?'

'You worked on me, and you set Jimmy on my daughter. You want to get her to come to your church.'

'David, you've got me all wrong.'

'And you've got us wrong if you think we're going to bother with your ridiculous church service. You may still wish to fill your head with kids' stories, but Bianca is far too mature to be interested.'

'I thought you just said she was just a child…'

He was right, and he was wrong, but it was far too complicated to explain, and I was on the verge of going volcanic. My throat was starting to hurt, so I just glared at him, and walked away. But he followed me:

'David, what on earth is your problem?' he shouted as I paced away from him. Now he was pretty heated too. 'I understand that you've had some pretty rotten Christmases in the past, but you can't let it dominate your life.'

I stopped dead at those words, and slowly turned on my heels. The man who had betrayed me, and whose son had crossed the line with my nearest and dearest, had now really pushed my button.

'Really Mark? And what would you know about it?' I walked back towards him, and put a fence between us. 'You've got a nice job, a nice wife, a nice big house that's all yours. Now imagine that one day, someone took away your job, and your wife left you, near enough within

24 hours. And imagine that because of those two things, you couldn't afford to pay for the house and had to rent out most of the rooms to complete strangers, and cook them breakfast every day. Imagine that Mark. Now would that day – the one on which you lost almost everything you cared about – come to represent a happy anniversary for you? Would you want to sing songs, eat food, and celebrate with as many people as possible on that day?'

Mark was speechless. I had more in the tank:

'Do you know when I start thinking about Christmas? Do you know when I start worrying about how desperately sick I'll feel on that day and those around it? Boxing Day. I think about it all the time.'

'But David,' Mark piped eventually, 'you can't dwell on the past for your whole life. It's not fair on Bianca – it's not even fair on you.'

'Well that's all nice sentiment Mark, and nothing I haven't heard before, but thanks anyway.'

Mark's eyes were sad. I wondered for a moment whether I'd got him wrong after all, but then corrected myself. We both stayed quiet for a while – he was contemplative, I was taking a breath – and then he tried a different line:

'What would make it better?' he asked.

'If my wife hadn't gone mad and left me, I could probably have coped with the rest,' I replied.

'What about this Christmas? What would make this Christmas better?'

I thought for a moment. It'd certainly be better if we were in the Caribbean, or if I'd managed to track down one of those blasted video game things. Then I looked down at my lifeless hand, and held it up.

'I'd be happier if I didn't have to go through Christmas with one functioning arm,' I said. 'At least then it would only be as bad as usual.'

Then I slinked away, to contemplate a worse Christmas than last year.

I was lying on my bed, writing the above, when Bianca burst in, wearing her father's best angry face. As I could have predicted, she came to lambaste me for my performance on her 'boyfriend's' front step. I pointed out that she was far too young for 'boyfriends', and she exclaimed that she was 'thirteen for goodness sake' (which I already knew). Then I angrily explained that we were being taken for a very big ride: that our neighbours had mistaken us for a turn-of-the-century African tribe and were trying to shepherd us into their out-of-date religion. Then she searched her vocabulary for a word meaning 'cynic', and I exclaimed that I didn't care what she thought of me now and that she'd be thanking me later. Then she started to cry a bit, and screeched something about going to a carol service with Jimmy on

Sunday. Then, completely vindicated, I grounded her. One of the doctors banged on the joining wall, and my daughter told me that she hates me before departing in a river of tears. Then I slunk away, to contemplate a worse Christmas than the worst Christmas ever.

Saturday
20th December

Sometimes, things happen that you can't explain. A flock of birds designates your windscreen as a toilet, while leaving every other car in the street alone. Or a pop song, with all the quality and musicianship of a two-year-old playing My First Banjo, gets to number one in the pop charts. Things like that just don't make any rational sense, and yet they still happen. This morning, when I woke up, I discovered something just as inexplicable.

My hand was better. I could move all the fingers; I could feel the wrist flexing behind the plaster. To say the least, this represents an unexpectedly quick recovery. To say a little more, it equates to a minor miracle.

That wasn't my first thought – of course. My first thought was that the sleep-deprived doctor who'd treated me after my little fridge-punching incident had made a rather crucial error, and treated a bruise or sprain as a break. But that wasn't his assessment this morning, when I made an uninvited appearance at his hospital. In fact, he had the x-rays to prove it.

'Mr Street,' he said, looking through his heavy eyelids in disbelief, 'you seem to have mended quite remarkably. I see these x-rays, taken just moments after you . . . '

'Walked into a door,' I reminded him.

'Yes,' he yawned. 'These x-rays show a clean break. Now, twelve days later, the hand is showing no damage whatsoever. If I hadn't seen you myself in both cases, I wouldn't believe it to be true.'

The images were surprising, but conclusive. I looked to the doc for help, but noticed that he was starting to nod off.

'How do you explain it then doctor?' I hollered, waking him instantly.

'Er . . . I don't know if I can Mr Street. Are you a religious man?'

'Certainly not!' I snapped, possibly a little too wildly.

'Then we'll have to put it down to a triumph of mind over matter. What we call psychosomatic healing. You seem to have willed yourself better.'

This satisfied me for the walk home, but not for much longer. The truth is, I'm not one of the world's most positive thinkers. I didn't want a broken hand, but I was much more interested in getting depressed about it and feeling sorry for myself than I was in generating positive energy to mend it. So either I have supremely powerful thought energy, and should join some sort of circus, or my other conclusion comes into play.

But why would a miracle happen to a man like me?

Oh, by the way, in other news, the reign of telephonic terror continues:

'David, it's Louisa again. I'm worried about you. I spoke to Dr McKenzie, and he says he hasn't seen you all month. You know you're supposed to go to your sessions David. I'm still going to mine. I know it's difficult David, but it helps. You're not ready to stop yet David; Dr McKenzie says he wants you to come back, but you've been ignoring all his calls too. Please give me a call back David. I just want to know that you're OK. I want to know that Bianca's OK. Call me.' Beep.

Sunday
21st December

It's six o'clock in the evening, and I'm lying on my bed again. If I'm honest, I've spent most of the last three years here. Not because I was sick – at least, not because I was physically sick. It's just that, most days, I've not been able to find the motivation to get up and move around my futile little existence.

I'd felt a little revived of late though. Bianca has grown to be quite intelligent for such a young girl, and I've sometimes been contented by just watching her grow. The conversations we've had over weekend takeaways have occasionally been dazzling. One time we stayed up all night talking about places we'll go when we win the lottery. Another time, back in the summer, we sat in the garden all evening making up stories. She and I have been getting close.

But I couldn't expect it to last forever. If you're watching something beautiful bloom and grow, you've got to expect that sooner or later someone else is going to notice that beauty and take it away. Now that's exactly what's happened. And even if I'm partly to blame, I have to realise that I was only ever the gardener.

So now Bianca, having completely ignored my attempt to ground her, is sitting in a church service with the family next door. Then she'll go carol singing – of all things, it's like a knife to my heart – and if I'm lucky I'll see her for a split-second around ten. I shan't hold out hope. In fact, I think I'll probably just stay here on the bed until someone needs breakfast.

You know, I said once, somewhere on these pages, that I used to quite like Christmas. I wasn't joking, although it must be quite hard to believe from everything I've said. Honestly though, Christmas used to be great. But then Christmas is great if you've got a job and a happy family.

Christmas day, five years ago. We were still in our old flat, on the other side of town, and since the mortgage was so low we had bags of money – pots of the stuff – so much that it seems ridiculous now. Louisa was a high-flier; I was earning big commission. We'd bought each other outlandish gifts, spent the sort of money on food and decoration that would make Geoff next door blush, and turned the whole month of December into one long party. I even had a Santa costume (although not a robot to fill it).

We'd managed to avoid having any of Louisa's awful family there, and for the first and only time it was just Bianca, Louisa and me. It was perfect – I still remember the whole thing vividly. Bianca woke around six, as little girls do, and despite our pretend protestations she was ripping through wrapping at the end of our bed by quarter past. There were toys, games, craft kits, teddy bears, sweets, clothes and little pieces of cute plastic jewellery. She was still going at eight o'clock – it's a wonder that morning alone didn't turn her into a slobbering materialistic greed monster. Louisa and I swapped gifts too – most of them in smaller boxes, but no less extravagant. Diamond studded jewellery, expensive perfumes and £100-a-bottle Parisian skincare treatments – and those were just her presents to me. I bought her a car, for goodness sake. These days I can barely afford to put petrol in one.

At ten o'clock – and you may have trouble with this bit – we skipped down to the local chapel for a quick feelgood service. Bianca took a new doll with her, Louisa wore new earrings, and the vicar even commented on my pleasant aroma. We sang a few songs, and kept catching one another's eyes as we did so. It was all we could do to stop ourselves from giggling at any point. We were so happy.

Back for lunch – prepared by yours truly – and a no-expense-spared meal of decadence. We didn't have turkey like other people. We had wild pheasant, no less. And a box of those crackers from that London department store which contain seriously good prizes and tear-proof party hats.

The rest of the day was a mass of Christmas television, board games and more food. Then we went to bed, got up and did most of it again on Boxing Day.

And when you've loved Christmas that much, it's a lot easier to hate it as much as I do now.

OK, so the magic mended arm was one thing. But what happened today was quite another. And now what I want to know is this: is someone up there planning a preposterously elaborate joke at my expense? Are these merely the opening gambits in some sort of cosmic four-move checkmate?

So I'm cleaning the rooms this afternoon. Usually Bianca does it, but she seems to be on leave at the moment and it's hard to find a good temp at short notice when you're only paying 50p an hour. I start with the two twin rooms housing our three men of letters, and discover – via the medium of illegal rummaging – that they're psychologists, here for a three-week conference on depression. Aha! No wonder they've been giving me a wide birth – they probably need cheering up in their free time – not another case study.

I finish up in there, then I move on to what seems to have been designated the odd-smelling room – the two-and-a-half bed joint currently being inhabited by three country boys. Last month, an old woman was giving it a cabbagey odour. This month, it's a heady mix of training shoes, instant just-add-water snacks and farm. I clean it quickly and sparingly, because frankly, what's the point?

Finally, I open the door to Hector's little writing den, to discover that . . . he's disappeared. Either that, or he's been transformed by aliens into a small box and an envelope. I open the envelope, just to check, and to my shocked relief find that he's left behind enough cash to pay for the room for the rest of the month. And what's more, he's written me a little note:

> Just a little note to say,
> I'm sorry you hate Christmas.
> I hope this box will cheer you up,
> And nothing rhymes with Christmas.

Cute (I'll forgive him and assume he had to write that one in a hurry).

Obviously, having read that work of genius, there's only one option left open to me. I pick up the box and shake it. It doesn't rattle, or explode, both of which are a good thing. So then I open it, and inside, find something which cannot possibly be staring me in the face. Hector has left me a Nagatoshi Gamemaster.

This is a little hard to explain, but I can't be entirely happy about the fact that Bianca's

dream Christmas present is now in my grasp.
It's not because she and I are currently engaging
in precious little conversation – I was still
always going to get her a present, whatever
happened. No, I'm unhappy because if there's
one thing I really hate – more than anything at
all – it's people who get away without paying.
And here am I, with expensive electronic gold
dust in my hands, given to me by a man who I
abused throughout his stay in my home. And a
bag full of money which I haven't earned. I've
become the thing I hate the most. Back to bed.

So here I am again, in my big, big, half-empty
bed. I've had so many great times in here. All of
them while asleep.

I've had some rough times here too. Close to
three years worth. Put here by one bad
Christmas, and shackled here by the ache I feel
every time I think about it – which is basically
every time I think. And do you know why?

Because we were so close. So close to everything we'd talked about, dreamed about and
saved for. So close to being a perfect family,
with everything we needed; with security; with
happiness. And on our way to nearly getting
there – as we strived and strived, as Louisa flew
high and I shot hot – we got distracted by all the
money, and all the competition, and we
changed. I became downbeat and distrustful,
and struggled to find a good word to say

about another human being, and she became irrational and neurotic, and struggled to find a good word to say about me. We were nearly there though. We put down the deposit on the big house, and we got Bianca into the good school, and we booked the very expensive holiday to Jamaica. But what we didn't realise was that we'd also moved in to a giant house of cards. One day I walked in to J P Truelove associates, and someone ripped out the King of Diamonds. One day later, there were a whole lot of cards on the floor, but no Queen.

I know we were in a bad way, but I can't help wondering how things might have worked out differently if I hadn't lost my job that Christmas. Bianca might still be here with me, instead of out with the carol singers for the second night in a row, and Louisa might still be my wife, instead of my regular crank telephone caller.

And here she is again:

'David. It's nearly Christmas and I'm going to ask you to do just one thing for me. We had a lot of good times together. We brought a beautiful girl into the world together. You were my best friend and the love of my life. Now remember all that when I ask you to do this one thing. And before you do, listen to this: I am sorry about that tacky gift set I left on your doorstep. I'm sorry about all the things I've left there in the past too. All the self-help books, and the tacky novelties, and the parcels of foods I know you hate. I'm sorry for all of it; I only did it because I knew it would irritate you; I only wanted to irritate you because I can't stand the fact that you ignore me. I'm still unhappy David – you know I am. It still hurts as much as it did on the day I left you. But this is just making it worse. So please, please David, all I ask is this: pick up the telephone, give me a call, and let me know that you're OK. Let me know that you're both OK. Then, I promise, I'll leave you alone. I won't call again. Please.' Beep.

For a moment today, I thought about it. I thought about calling her up, just to see what would come out of my mouth when she answered. But I thought too long, and after that it was never an option.

This town doesn't usually attract visitors of a high calibre. All we've got here is a load of the same shops that everywhere else has got, plus an abnormally high number of cemeteries and a pub on every corner. So in terms of tourism, people generally only come here to trace their family or get drunk. There are exceptions of course, like our three doctors, here for a conference, or the occasional wedding / will reading guests, but other than that the Streets Ahead Guesthouse is like any of the other B & B's round here: visited by middle-aged people looking to find some roots, or by young people looking to cut loose from them.

So why today a visitor in very expensive trousers decided to embody an extraordinary break from the norm is completely beyond my comprehension at this time. But she did.

The doorbell rang at around four, and after my cries for someone else to answer were not graced with a response, I reluctantly ventured downstairs. Behind the door was a petite, slim girl of about twenty-five, hidden behind dark glasses and a big floppy hat. As I looked at her then for the first time, there stirred within me a flash of half-recognition, but as I don't know any attractive young women, I dismissed the thought almost as quickly as it had arrived.

'Have you got a room here please?' she asked, in an American-accented voice that was also strangely familiar.

'Of course!' I squeaked, as you sometimes do when you haven't spoken all day. 'Come on through.'

I showed her to the room recently vacated by Hector Malone, and offered to make her a cup of tea. She accepted, and I retreated to the kitchen.

As I waited for the kettle to boil, I decided to steal a few moments of neighbourhood watch before it got too dark. To my left, Geoff was up a ladder, fixing a giant 'Merry Christmas' sign to his roof. To my right, Mark and his family (plus half of mine) were locked away. Ah, this was more interesting though: in the middle of the road, directly in front of our house, there was a massive off-road van with two huge men in the front. Perhaps I was about to discover the real reason for Hector's rapid departure.

The kettle started to whistle at me. I was intrigued by what was outside, and so kept one eye on the van as I made the familiar-looking girl's tea. This possibly explains why I subsequently spilt tea on the floor. Annoyed, I reached for the first absorbent object I could find to mop it up, and happened to pick up the Christmas TV guide. And as the brown liquid began to soak through its pages, I suddenly saw something even more amazing than the FBI assault vehicle outside my window. The front cover picture showed a couple embracing on a ship's deck, trailing the big Christmas movie. Now I knew where I'd seen the new girl before, and the hat, glasses and bodyguards instantly made sense.

I barged into the bedroom with half a cup of tea in my hand, to find one of the world's biggest movie stars trimming her toenails on a lumpy bed.

'You're Andrea Andrews!' I blubbered.

'Yes,' she said, continuing to clip.

' 'Why on earth have you come here?' (I mean, I like this town as much as the next man who lives here, but it's hardly Beverley Hills.)

'I'm doing this movie in Britain next year,' she said, wrestling with the nail of her big toe. 'It's about a British girl who works in a little hotel like this one.'

'Does she fall in love with a loveable posh guest?'

'No, she goes on a killing spree. It's a bit of a girly film really. So anyway, they sent me here to research the role. And Christmas was the only time I could fit it in to my schedule. So here I am, on my own.'

'On your own, apart from the two human guard dogs in the van?'

'Oh, those two? They're on two hundred dollars an hour each just to sit there. You won't hear a peep out of them.'

'Great. Here's your tea.' I said, as the words 'huge' and 'tip' rushed to the forefront of my brain.

'Thanks. Say – do you have a list of local restaurants that might be open on Christmas Day?'

'Of course!' I lied, and ran off to find the phone book.

I can't quite believe that Andrea Andrews has chosen this town and this establishment to rest her famous little head in. It makes less sense than Hector's decision to reward me for my nastiness; less even than the fact that I'll have two working hands when it comes to carving the turkey. People like her do not come to places like this.

It's times like this that not having any friends hurts the hardest. Imagine being able to say to people: 'Andrea Andrews is in my bedroom.' I should be on the phone right now, not writing it down in a book that no one will ever read.

Wednesday 24th December

There's only one way to explain how things ended up like they did. I'll just have to tell you the whole story.

It's about nine o'clock, and I'm in an empty house. My daughter – the only good thing in my life – has not spoken to me since Friday and, to make matters far worse, is indulging in one of the world's most despicable pastimes of all with a bunch of woolly-hatted old people. Then she'll be off to church, and as far as that's concerned, I'd rather she was at a nightclub. Christmas is barely three hours away, and I'm even lonelier than usual. I'm sinking fast, back towards the depths of depression, just when I thought I'd clawed my way out.

I've got a great Christmas present for a girl who's likely to throw it back in my face, no food in the house besides egg, bacon, mushrooms and sausage, no decorations, no tree, and now no TV guide. There's still only one card on the shelf, my advent calendar has been in the bin for days, and I'm feeling so terrorised by my ex-wife's messages that I've unplugged the phone. Facing facts, I've hit an all-time Christmas low, and with my history, that's not an easy thing to achieve.

Then things get even worse. Mark appears at the living room window and spots me sitting there even though I've turned the lights out. He taps on the glass for three minutes until I eventually respond. I let him in, invite him coldly to sit down, but don't turn on the lights.

'David,' he says calmly. 'Polly and I are worried about you.'

I nod my head, because the fight has gone from my body now.

'We've seen a lot of Bianca lately,' he continues. 'Which means that you haven't. She told us that you've been arguing.'

He pauses, and chews over his next words like something hard to swallow. I look out of the window.

'Bianca told us something,' he goes on. 'In confidence. She told us that after you split up with your wife, you had to go and see someone. A doctor of some sort. She says you saw him for nearly three years, but that sometime last month you stopped going.'

(All this was correct, and sorry for not mentioning it at the start. When life fell apart, I did the same. I got very depressed – if it hadn't been for Bianca I would have seriously considered ending it all. Then I started seeing Dr

McKenzie, and while things didn't hurt any less, I gained a little perspective and managed to hold my life together again. But I'd been seeing him for three years, and I was seriously starting to lose my self-respect. I was getting dependent. So last month, I decided to go cold turkey and make it on my own. I don't like to admit this, but it seems patently obvious now that I wasn't capable of doing so.)

Again, my only response to Mark is a barely-committed nod.

'David, you've got yourself into a bit of a mess mate. You've fallen out with your daughter – and I know how much she means to you because you told me; you misunderstood me, your friend, and now we're not talking either. It's Christmas Eve, and the whole world is either out partying or in with their friends and family, and you're here, in the dark, on your own.'

At last I open my mouth:

'Well thanks for that assessment Mark, I feel whole lot better now. Shall we go to church to give thanks?'

'David, you've still got it all wrong. I like you. I really do. I've found it hard making friends since we moved here, but you seemed like someone I could really get on with. You're real, you're down-to-earth. You don't buy into all this materialistic rubbish that everyone else is so concerned with. I really connect with that.

And that's why I'm here – not because I think I have some quick-fix answer to your problems, or because I want to get you to think the same way as I do – it's because I'm worried about you.'

'And you think I should start seeing Dr McKenzie again? You think that will make it all better, if I go back to my old crutch?'

'Maybe it will David, maybe it won't. Only you know that. But I'm here now because it's not too late to save your Christmas.'

'What?'

'Go and find Bianca, and tell her how much she means to you. Then tomorrow, you'll wake up and it'll be a new day, just like any other. Forget that it's Christmas – just spend the day together, give her a present, and tell her that you love her.'

I think about it for a minute. It seems like a good idea for a while, but then I realise that it would involve driving around the streets on Christmas Eve, watching thousands of people celebrating in the glare of a million multi-coloured lights. So I say:

'I'll think about it Mark. Now I think you should probably go home.'

An hour later, I'm still home alone. Then I hear heavy brakes outside, followed, a full five minutes later, by a key in the lock. Andrea Andrews has returned. But she's not alone.

'Excuse me, sir?' she calls, assuming there's no one in the front room.

'Hello!' I exclaim, leaping into the hallway to find that Andrea is accompanied by two teenagers, one of whom has been drinking heavily, and the other of whom is heavily pregnant.

'Are there any other rooms available?' asks Andrea. 'These two need somewhere to stay.'

I look at the bloated girl, who can't be more than three years older than Bianca. She's propping up what I assume is her boyfriend, although it really should be the other way around.

'I'm sorry,' I say. We're fully booked.

'Well do you know anywhere else they could go?' She's getting all maternal now.

'Afraid not. We're the only place around here that takes Christmas guests.' My voice drops to a whisper: 'I hope you don't find me rude, but where exactly did you find these two?' ('These two' are now sitting on the stairs, looking anxious.)

'They followed me. I was taking a stroll home from your local pub . . . '

'But I heard the van . . . '

'They followed me too. I'm walking home, and these two spot me. They ask me for an autograph, he tries to kiss me, and then they ask me where I'm staying. I tell them, and then they cross the road and follow me on the other sidewalk.' She starts to laugh as she speaks. 'I think they thought they were being subtle. Have you ever seen a very pregnant girl and a wasted guy trying to be subtle? It's great, believe me.'

I walk to the two slumped bodies at the foot of my stairs.

'So,' I say, 'sounds like you've been playing a game of "Stalk the Star".'

'We weren't stalking her,' says the girl defensively. 'We just followed her to find a place to stay.'

'Well you can't stay here. There's no room.'

The girl starts to sob. Then she explains that she's eight-and-a-half months gone, and that she and her boyfriend have come here to run away from angry parents. Andrea begins to plead with me, which, considering she earns $20 million per movie, is quite an experience. But there really is no room, and I explain that in no uncertain terms. I agree however, that they can stay for an hour to warm up and share a drink. I'm not completely heartless, after all.

Then my quiet night alone disintegrates like a paper space shuttle attempting re-entry.

'I think my waters just broke,' is just about the last thing you want to hear from a stranger sitting in your favourite armchair. But that's what she says, in a sort of terrified shriek. I've just returned from the kitchen, where Porky's boyfriend has just passed out on the floor, and this piece of news doesn't help my mood.

Nevertheless, from somewhere I find a sudden drive, probably brought on by the feeling of usefulness that's overcoming me. I reach for the telephone and call for an ambulance, but I get the 'busiest night of the year' spiel and a one-hour arrival estimate. Then I run to the car, but remember the eight whiskies and think again. Andrea goes out to find her bodyguards, but discovers that they've sneaked off for the night. Geoff's drunk; Mark's gone to church. Basically, it's down to us.

Well, us and the three young farmers, who've heard the neighbourhood gossip about a world-wide pin-up staying in their B & B, and pack into the front room just as things get messy. Our pregnant teenager looks like she's ready to explode. She's certainly making all the right noises.

'This may sound like a stupid question,' I say rather agitatedly, 'but has anyone here ever been at a birth?'

'I have!' slurs one of the young farmers. 'I've seen my dad do loads of calves!'

The soon-to-be mum gives out a blood-curdling roar, and I realise that I'm going to have to be the midwife here. But just then I spot a chance of a reprieve. The front door clicks open again, and my other three guests return from their evening on the town.

'You three! Get in here now!' I shout, at a volume not reached since my rugby days.

Three heads pop themselves through the doorway. 'Oh my!' says one of them.

'We've got an emergency!' I say, like I've seen them do on television. 'This girl's about to give birth. She needs your help.'

All three heads shrink back, and suddenly they're talking to me from the safety of the corridor.

'Why us? Why can't you do it?' says a muted voice.

'Because you're all doctors, and I'm a depressive hotelier.'

'But we're not medical doctors!'

Right. Forgot that. So I'm back into the breach once more. Andrea brings towels, the young farmers all crack open a beer, and I wish that Bianca was here.

Somehow, ten minutes later, I'm watching a mother cradle her newborn child, as farmers and thinkers clink glasses around me and a world-famous movie star rests her tearful head on my shoulder. That's not something you can say every day.

'Why are you crying?' I ask Andrea.

She blows her nose on a handkerchief that probably cost more than my car, and looks up at me.

'Because it's so incredible. You just helped to bring new life into the world. And at Christmas too.' Then she splutters: 'But that's not all. I'm crying too because this reminds me of how unhappy I am. And how trapped I feel being an actress when really I've always wanted to be something else.'

'A mother?'

'No. A nurse. I always wanted to be a nurse. When I was a kid I always dreamed of working in a hospital – making people feel better, and helping babies to be born. I even started training, but I was acting in my spare time, and it was the acting that took off. Then the money got in the way, and now I can never go back to it.'

'Why not?'

'Because I'm an actress.'

'But you don't want to be. Why don't you stop being an actress and start being a nurse?'

'Could I do that?'

'Well of course you can! You can't let money rule your life. You've got to make the best of things regardless of money. Money ruined my life.'

'It did?'

'Yeah. So don't let it ruin yours. Be a nurse, if that's what you really want.'

So then Andrea Andrews, world famous former actress and new trainee nurse, throws her arms around me and kisses me on the cheek. Then she goes to hug the teenager in the middle of the room who's just changed her life.

And then everything freezes. Everything stops, and it's just me, standing there on my own, surrounded by smiling people. And suddenly, after all that frenzied activity, I begin to see and think more clearly. Every event of the last 24 days begins to play through my mind in sequence, as if I'm five seconds from death. I see the bad stuff first – like my fights with Bianca, my argument with Mark, my broken hand and my terrifying bus journey to town. But then I see the good stuff too. I see good times with Bianca, and with Mark. I see my mended hand, and the gift from Hector. And then I see what's just happened, right before my eyes, with the Hollywood heroine and the frightened teenagers. Miracles have been happening to the left, right and centre of my life for the last week, and I've been too stubborn to acknowledge any of them. Finally, with my head about to burst and my heart not far behind, I hear again the words of Mark:

'Go and find Bianca, and tell her how much she means to you. Then tomorrow, you'll wake up and it'll be a new day, just like any other. Forget that it's Christmas – just spend the day together, give her a present, and tell her that you love her.'

Barely a moment later, I've grabbed my shoes and coat and I'm off and running.

The trouble with St Mark's on the Hill is, for the unfit man, fairly obvious from the name of the place. So with the service in full swing inside, I spend a few moments catching my breath on the wall outside.

. I'm not much of a churchgoer, for reasons that are probably quite clear. But the last time I was inside a church was at Christmas, so I only feel as guilty as the rest of the British population about returning now. From what I remember though, there's not much opportunity for talking during the service, which will make reconciliation with my estranged daughter quite difficult. I think about writing something apologetic on a piece of paper and handing it to her. Then I consider a well-scripted whisper. And then I look at my watch, notice that it's two minutes to twelve, and walk in without a plan.

As I stagger down the aisle, looking around desperately like a lost child in a supermarket, they're singing 'O Come All Ye Faithful' (clearly, in welcoming me with that song, they've got the wrong guy). Every pair of eyes is being tempted away from the hymnsheets by the arrival of my dishevelled self, and help-ful-looking ushers are hurrying towards me from every angle. On the front row, I notice Mark, singing his heart out as any good Rugby Man should. Next to him is his wife; next to them are their children. And next to them is a pretty little girl with braided hair, and one empty seat.

As I draw level with Bianca, the song goes into its stirring final verse. 'Sing choirs of

angels, sing in exultation!' cries the church, as
my daughter and I look one another in the eyes
for once. The pitch and the volume are rousing,
and give me the strength to reach out a hand.
She ignores it, and throws herself hard towards
me, nearly knocking me off balance. Then I hold
her for a while, with such joy on my face that the
organist feels inspired to improvise another
verse of the hymn.

We walk almost all the way home in silence,
until I pluck up the courage to break it. We stop
in the street, and I put my hands on her shoulders.

'Tomorrow,' I say, 'we're going to have a
proper Christmas. I've got you a present, and
we'll improvise with dinner. I'll even try to
make some decorations.'

Bianca beams and buries herself in my coat. I
pull her back:

'But there's one thing I want to ask you. Just
one thing, which you won't like.'

She looks a little apprehensive, but listens.

'I've barely spoken to your mum for the last
three years. I know that's because of what she
did, and I know you're still as hurt as I am. But
we haven't moved anywhere. We haven't
moved on for three years, and we're still
pumping out all this hatred because of what
happened.'

Bianca looks upset, but nods.

'I know you think you hate her, but a lot of that is because of the way I've made you. I think it's time that we stopped blaming her, and realise that it was my fault too.'

'What?'

'Your mum and I split up because we argued, and we argued because of money. She left us because she couldn't take any more shouting – because I was a tiny bit more resilient than she was. But she hates herself for what happened – more I think than we ever hated her. She calls us every day, because she wants someone to say I forgive you, or it's OK. But no one ever answers, and she has to keep crying out and lashing out and hating.'

Bianca is having trouble with this. In some far more difficult way, this is a little like telling her that Santa doesn't exist. I'm trying to explain that everything I've filled her head with for three years was wrong. Her lip is quivering as a result.

'Your mum leaves presents for me. Most of them are nasty little things, designed to upset me. But this month she left something different on the front step – a diary that I've been filling in for the whole of December. The idea was that you wrote down your experiences over Christmas, in order somehow to find some true meaning in the midst of it all. And although I never ever thought it would work, I think I've discovered something. Christmas isn't about money, or presents . . . '

Bianca's face falls further.

' . . . although I've got you an absolutely brilliant present this year . . . '

Bianca's face lights up.

'Christmas is about love, and family, and realising what's important.'

'So what do you want to ask me?' enquires a confused but beautiful thirteen-year-old with braided hair.

'I want to invite your mum over for Christmas dinner,' I reply.

Then she begins to cry, gently at first, and then like the newborn baby that's being loaded into an ambulance in the next street. I bite my cheek with nervousness as she slowly lifts her hand, and then, as she raises her thumb, I sweep her off her feet and cry just as much.

Thursday
25th December

So there you have it. Against all the odds, I've found some sort of reason for the season, and it's not all looking quite as meaningless as it used to. The television is still terrible, and people are still money mad and mostly artificial, but there are little flecks of light in the prevailing gloom. And some of the credit for the change in my mood must go to you, Mr Diary. Writing it down helped me to think, and thinking helped me to get my daughter back. While today wasn't the best Christmas I've ever had, it certainly wasn't the worst one either.

Thanks then, for being there when no one else was, and for arriving right on time. At first you seemed like a piece of worthless seasonal tat, and a waste of good woodland. But now I've realised that you were never quite what you seemed to be . . .

I sit across the table from my wife for the first time in exactly three years. Our daughter is there too, but she's more interested in her new toy than her eerily-resurrected family

Christmas of the past. Louisa is wiping her eyes sporadically with a tissue, and I'm feeling strangely serene.

For most of the afternoon we just sit. My radical retake on the traditional Christmas lunch – roast sausage and bacon with egg and mushroom stuffing – goes down surprisingly well, and Bianca even digs out three secret crackers that she's kept hidden under her bed for years. But the situation is so unusual, so novel, so strangely comforting, that we're mostly content to sit together in quietness.

We do have one conversation however, where I attempt to forgive her for the Magico™ debacle. Her response is, to say the least, unexpected:

'You know,' I say, 'that box of Christmas stuff was actually quite funny.'

'Really?' she asks, surprised that I could find anything festive even remotely amusing. 'I thought you'd hate it. That's why I put it there.'

We both laugh a little.

'The advent calendar was pretty cute. It lasted most of the month, until it just degenerated into commercials.'

'Thought you'd like that bit.'

'But the diary. The diary was actually pretty good. I wrote in it almost every day, and that's not like me at all. It wasn't all that bad for a piece of cynically marketed and almost certainly overpriced tat. It's one of the reasons we're all sitting here like this now . . . '

And then I stopped, because I realised that Louisa didn't understand a single word I was saying. And then she said:

'What diary David? I didn't buy you a diary.'

So Who Did? – An Afterword

[Before we go any further, I need to be completely open-handed. The fiction is at an end, and what we've arrived at now is an extended author's note. It talks about the novel that you've just read; in some ways it may help to better explain that novel. But it is not a part of it. So if you don't want to know why the author wrote David Street's Christmas Diary, and you don't particularly care what he was trying to say about life, love and Christmas through its pages, please stop reading now.]

In some ways, it's difficult to identify with David Street. He reads the *Daily Strange*, drinks Magna Cola, and watches John Van Schwarzkof movies – in other words, he lives in a fictional universe. He's also deliberately ageless and colourless, and resides in a town somewhere in England, although we have no idea which one. In fact, we don't even know for sure what decade he's living in. He's like nobody, because we just don't know enough about him to accurately compare him to anyone else.

And yet, David Street could be someone you know. You know people who struggle with Christmas because of the pain of divorce. You know people whose disappointment with themselves is balanced by the happiness they find in having raised a daughter or a son. You know parents desperate to purchase that special something without which Christmas would be a big disappointment.

And you know people who hate the materialism of Christmas almost as much as David Street. He is one of us, imperfect, battling against what life throws at him and trying as best he can to retain a sense of personal dignity and respect.

When we first meet David, we find him a familiar example of the perverseness of human nature – a man so desperately lonely, yet too stubborn to pick up the phone to call an ex-wife, repair relations with the daughter he loves, or accept the friendship of a genuine neighbour.

A man who would gladly improve the world around him, particularly at Christmas time, but who is reluctant to accept the promptings of his ex-wife, the badgering of his daughter, or the insights of a friend that might improve his desperate situation.

Some would argue that our hero (or anti-hero, depending on your viewpoint) is on the right road in despising the materialism of

Christmas, but fails to spot what it is all about. He sees the festival in the same way as the majority of people in Britain do. Most see Christmas as what society has made it: presents, food, parties, time with family, time off work. They love the romance of Christmas, and in some cases respect the tradition that surrounds it. Our celebration goes back to the pagan festival that celebrated the re-birth of the sun in Roman times. The 25th December was set as 'Christmas Day' by Pope Julius I in the fourth century AD. But it is just part of our folklore and tradition, nothing to do with them.

And then some go beyond this. They accept the religious undertones, and have little difficulty rehearsing the learn-and-repeat faith they memorised in their school days. Carols and readings never did anyone any harm, and if there's any truth to Christianity, Christmas is as good a time as any to keep your hand in. All of which is of course perfectly fine. People see life differently to one another. We live and let live.

David Street doesn't go this far. He sees Christmas as the root of every unhappiness in his life. He lost his wife at that time of year; he lost his job; he saw the money dry up – and worst of all he saw the whole country eating, drinking and being merry while his world spiralled down the toilet. So David can't live and let live – even in this society where intolerance is the greatest evil – because at this time of year, part of him doesn't even want to live at all.

As we watch the story unfold, we see several people trying to help David. His daughter, Bianca, loves him as much as he loves her, despite the tensions brought about by her age. His ex-wife, Louisa, who knows about his depression, and who shares it, keeps reaching out her hand to him despite constant rejection. Her persistence is almost supernatural, as is that of Mark – the friend next door who shows an unusual amount of forgiveness to his embittered neighbour. And then there's Hector Malone, the bad-poem-writing house guest to whom David shows such obvious disdain, but who comes running back like a loyal lapdog with an unexpected response. They're all doing their best to help David to get back on track and, of course, he can't see it. But quite what motivates them, considering the poison that so regularly spits from David's mouth, is something of a mystery.

Which brings us back to the final line of the story. Louisa left the box of festive rubbish on the doorstep, but she did not leave the diary, and it's diary-writing, more than any other factor, which brings about a change in David. So who left the diary?

There's a character in the story whose name is never mentioned. Yet his input is so great that in

Oscar terms we'd call him an actor, not a supporting actor. He's involved in every major scene in the plot, and yet he never shows his face. He's an orchestrator, working just out of view and moving all the chess pieces on the board of David's life.

He's the one who leaves the diary, and he's the one who heals David's arm. He brings the altruistic Hector to stay at the B & B, and gives Louisa and Mark their unnatural persistence. And because he knows David, and knows how much it will take to make him stop and think, he even sets up that ridiculously convoluted mirror of the nativity – complete with wise men, shepherds and miraculous star – right in his front room.

All this he does because he sees David's pain. He feels his deep depression, and sees the misery that he inflicts upon those closest to him. So he goes to quite incredible lengths to help him, because he cares so deeply about him.

The invisible character has quite considerable power – he can mend broken bones, obtain hard-to-get Christmas presents and even book a movie star at very short notice. Yet alongside all his power, he's also full of love. It takes a lot of loving patience to give someone like David a chance. It takes a lot of loving forgiveness to ignore David's bitterness and give him good things. It takes an awful lot of love to go to so much trouble.

David Street's Christmas Diary is a piece of original fiction. But the invisible character is borrowed from elsewhere. He's borrowed from another book – one which many people don't believe to be fiction. They think that it's a factual account of how the invisible character rescued the whole world, and strangely enough, it includes what some would call 'the true meaning of Christmas', that elusive thing that David – and many of us – secretly wants to find.

So stepping away from this book, and towards that one, there's a question to ask. If this character was real – this person who balances unthinkable power on one shoulder and unstoppable love on the other – would you want to meet and get to know him if you could?

Looking around today, I believe that most people would. In the music charts, Robbie Williams cries out because he 'just wants to feel real love'. In movies like *Star Wars* and *The Matrix*, everyone is looking for a 'chosen one' to come and save them from their desperate situations. Deep down, it seems like we're all searching for something beyond the three dimensions of our natural reality, even if we don't know what it is. This invisible character, if he's real, could really fit the bill.

Some people, like me, believe that he is real, and that he can be met and known. And that, in the all-too-American words of Magico™, is the 'reason for the season'.

Two thousand years ago, a baby was born in Israel, in very unspectacular surroundings. The parents named him Jesus, and he lived – teaching, influencing and performing miracles – until he reached his mid-thirties, when he was sentenced to death – unjustly – for being a serious troublemaker. (And if you don't believe that, perhaps you should examine whether you believe in the existence of say, Julius Caesar, or William the Conqueror, and why. There's as much historical evidence for Christ's existence as there is for most of the other great figures who we teach our children about. Unless you want to get involved in one mighty conspiracy theory, it's probably worth accepting that someone called Jesus did exist back then, even if he wasn't quite what he said he was.)

Anyway, all this we've heard before. We learned it as children, we got cynical about it in our early teens, and thereafter it probably never seemed like more than a nice story for keeping children sweet. And somehow, the greatest revolutionary who ever lived – who healed the broken, raised the dead and somehow came back to life after a gruesome and torturous death – has been anaesthetised by modern society. Somehow, 'Jesus' has become a rather embarrassing word. (In 1,000 years time, will people feel awkward when they speak the name of Gandhi or Mandela?) We've managed to convince ourselves that he's completely irrelevant.

So, we make merry at Christmas because we get to give and receive presents, eat obscenely calorific food, and drink ourselves into a stupor. What was once the celebration of the birth of history's greatest and most important figure, has now become a celebration of every kind of gluttony. And when you think of it like that, it's not hard to sympathise with someone as cynical as David Street.

But what happens to David in this story is exactly what really happened to the whole of humanity at Christmas. The invisible character (God) saw that we were making a complete mess of things – hurting ourselves and each other at almost every opportunity – and he intervened in order to set us back on the right track. He sent his son (Jesus), who was every bit as powerful as himself, and put him among us on the earth as a simple man, as vulnerable as the rest of us. That's what the Bible (the other book I was referring to earlier) says, anyway. And while it's fair to object to the authority and reliability of a book passed down through the ages by human hands, it's from the Bible that we draw every other aspect of the Christmas story – the bits we happily accept because they don't threaten the comfort-zones of our lives.

And that's probably why we've pumped Christmas full of anaesthetic. We like the nice story, with the donkey and the star, but we'd rather ignore all the other stuff if that's OK. But the trouble is that when we truly examine the message of Christmas, it becomes quite hard to ignore the other stuff. Because if Jesus, this man who walked around Israel 2,000 years ago, was God in human form, then the wider Christmas message deserves rather more attention than we may give it. Intervention at great cost is generally front page news, whether it's a buy-out of a company about to go bust, a kidney donation to a dying child, or a rescue of captured soldiers. If the Bible claims that God came to earth to somehow rescue us from something, it might be a good idea to try to understand why he did it, and what our response to that should be, even if we choose to ignore both.

The message of the Bible is that the problems in our human nature are not just irritations that drive us to distraction and wind up our nearest and dearest; they are one of the repercussions of us ignoring God. If at this point you are thinking, well I don't believe in God, you might reflect on what (or which) God it is that you don't believe in, and what sort of God you would like to believe in.

God (the Bible God) is our creator, and despite the fact that we generally ignore him, he still really likes us. In fact, he loves us – unconditionally, in the same way that David Street loves his daughter Bianca, and better. Therefore he wants us to have good things, or at least, those things that he in his infinite wisdom knows to be good for us. This may rule out a fast car or a huge pay rise, but it does include love, friendship, a better character and, most importantly, friendship with him and the promise of life after death.

Despite many people's protestations on this point, we do get a chance to hear and respond to this offer. And if we spend our whole lives celebrating Christmas and Easter, and never get round to asking why we're doing it, we're probably being a bit naïve. Generally though, we ignore the offer, and that's where all the anaesthetic makes it much easier.

But just as responding to God has excellent benefits, ignoring him has a gargantuan cost. When we choose to live in a God-free zone God says: 'Although it breaks my heart, I respect your choice, but beware that you will spend eternity without the good things I bring into the world.' (This includes: love, laughter, beauty, sex, sleep, holidays, good friends, wine.)

He doesn't want it to come to that. He wants to be our friend – in the genuine, best mate sense – and to prove he's serious, he sent his own son, Jesus Christ, to show us what living under his rule is like, and to hand us the invitation to be friends. So if the idea of a spiritual being you can't see – the invisible character in David

Street's life – freaks you out, don't worry. God says, look at the life of Jesus and you'll see the sort of God I am.

So leave aside for a moment the stuff you thought Christianity was about – attending church, doing charity work, giving money, abstaining from things you enjoy – and imagine for a moment knowing a God who wants the best for you and is prepared to work with you to make the changes you in your life that you want to make. How does that really sound?

At this point there's another, less comfortable point to make, and it's a pretty big one. God is also committed to changing stuff we didn't think needed changing. If you've ever left your car at the garage thinking you just needed an oil change, only to discover the whole engine needed an overhaul, you'll know what I mean.

It's not that God opts to make joining with him difficult, because he's 'difficult'. It's that we can't do it any other way. The engine always needed the work, even if you didn't know about it. You just would have driven along, blissfully unaware that anything was amiss, until one day it blew up in your face. We need work doing to us because deep down we know there is plenty wrong.

So if we are to be part of those who God has rescued we must recognise our desperate state, and be willing to hand our life over to him, by following the advice and teaching which he gives us in the Bible. And in this day and age, that probably sounds as appealing as a barbed wire sandwich. To most people Christianity appears to be about as out of touch and irrelevant as can be, with the Bible nothing but a rulebook for use in pooping parties and making you feel guilty. Blame the church for that, but don't let it fool you. The Bible is actually as applicable today as it was on its first print run – most of our laws and morals come directly from its pages, and it contains the greatest love story ever told: the story of a how a man laid down his life so that everyone else might live.

The reason Christians make so much of Jesus is that he showed us how to live life in the perfect, good for us way that God intends. He showed that it could be done. Christians make a lot of Christmas because they are pleased that he came. But they make even more of his life because his life was so special.

The Bible includes four eyewitness accounts (the gospels of Matthew, Mark, Luke and John) of how Jesus lived and the things he did so that we are in no doubt about the sort of person he was. God asks us to learn to live the kind of life Jesus lived – apart from his historical context of course – a real life, where we are, with our job and family, friends, neighbours and daily challenges.

At this point you may be surprised that I have not made a mention of the death of Jesus. It plays a crucial role, though once again the true meaning is sometimes missed.

The cross is the universal symbol of the church, the bridge between the chasm that exists between humanity on the one side and God on the other.

God's purity makes a relationship with him impossible unless someone bridges the gap. Jesus bridged the gap. On the cross Jesus was punished by God, in our place, for the whole ugly mass of stuff – the lies, the mistakes, the skeletons in all our closets – that separates us from him.

It's as if a list is made of all the stuff we have done wrong in our whole lives, in terms of thoughts, words, and actions. Even the 'nicest' of us could write one a mile long if we had to. God is perfect, and made us perfect, but all these things pile up and get in the way. So this list stands against us and prevents us from being near to God. And then Jesus comes along and wipes them all out, just for the sake of love.

The bit that most people find tricky is admitting that they need rescuing. Like David Street, we know we mess up, but we can't quite bring ourselves to believe that there's no hope for us.

If there is a God, we reason, he'll know we aren't so bad and accept us.

The best illustration of this sort of thinking has to be in the medical world. By and large we need to trust the doctors that the diagnosis is correct. We may not like it, but millions have become better by facing the bad news. It's the same in the spiritual realm. There's enough bad in us to condemn us. We are living way short of our potential now, and eternity is an awfully long time to regret not getting on God's side while we could.

By now you may well be expecting the sort of punch line our Christmas-hating hero faced from Mark. It's all driving towards the 'so what about you' sort of conclusion. Most of us can spot the hard sell and steel ourselves accordingly, whether it's the double-glazing salesman, or charity workers in the street.

So let me assure you that I understand any reticence to be convinced about Christianity because of an afterword at the end of a book. I, and millions of Christians may be wrong about this, and millions of others may be right to ignore 'God' after all. But why not check it out, just to be sure in your own mind, by reading one of the gospel accounts of the life of Jesus in the Bible? What have you to lose? At the very least you will be educated about a man who has affected the course of human history more than any other man, and at the best, you might find something that turns your life on its head.

You may have the impression that Christians badger people because they figure that they want other people to be as miserable as they are, or that they get a kick from labelling people 'sinners' so that they can feel superior. But the best examples of Christians are those who are simply like friends of yours who have stumbled across a bargain in the shops and want you to benefit. It has dawned on them that God's way does answer the longing of their hearts. They change their minds, receive God's forgiveness and friendship, and commit themselves to his way. Whatever else you may have heard, this is how the Bible defines being a Christian.

When my friends tell me about a good deal I am generally grateful. So David Street may have reacted badly to Mark, and this in itself may have felt like a hard sell, but be assured, the intention is genuine.

For if all this is true, and it works, and if life beyond death is godless without it, I think you'll agree it's worth looking into.

OTHER TITLES FROM AUTHENTIC LIFESTYLE

EAST END TO EAST COAST

Martin Saunders

An unlikely traveller.
An incredible journey.

When journalist Martin Saunders met champion weightlifter Arthur White, he had no idea what was around the corner. Arthur is a member of Tough Talk, a group of ex-hardmen from London's East End, whose lives have been radically and powerfully changed, and who now travel the world telling their stories.

Over the following six months, Martin hit the road with Tough Talk, following them from the picturesque mountains of France to the streets of a wounded New York. Along the way he uncovered countless amazing, shocking and amusing stories, made a few new friends, and watched as many lives were changed forever.

East End to East Coast is a book like no other. Part biography, part comedy travelogue, it charts the story of this amazing journey, while also asking some serious questions about masculinity and meaning.

ISBN: 1-86024-276-6   **Price: £5.99**

CHASED BY THE DRAGON
CAUGHT BY THE LAMB

Brian Morris with Martin Saunders

Staring down a police gun barrel and sick with cold turkey, Brian Morris had hit rock bottom. His life was in tatters, and a long spell in prison lay inevitably ahead. Yet somehow, this moment proved to be the turning point that saved and changed him for ever.

Join Brian as he gives a full and entertaining account of his life as an international drug dealer and long-term prisoner. Sometimes funny, sometimes shocking but always gripping, *Chased by the Dragon, Caught by the Lamb* is the amazing story of a man who finally found satisfaction in his search for the ultimate high.

ISBN: 1-86024-435-1   **Price: £6.99**